"The simplicity and directness of *The On-Purpose Person* really hits those of us who are striving for integration in our lives. Living the 'On-Purpose' life requires the kind of structure and encouragement that are provided in this book."

    —Steve S. Reinemund, former CEO, Peps
       of Business and Accountancy and the B
       Management, Professor of Leadership a
       University

"The secret of success is: Do more of what you're
not good at. That's what *The On-Purpose Person* is all about."

    —Stanley C. Olsen, Co-founder, Digital Equipment Corp.,
       Developer, Black Diamond Ranch

"What a refreshing book! To the point, and with the passion only a true believer can communicate, *The On-Purpose Person* should take its rightful place in every thinking person's bookcase."

    —Michael Gerber, CEO, The Michael Gerber Corporation,
       and Author, *The E-Myth*

"I love Kevin McCarthy's concept of being on-purpose."

    —Ken Blanchard, PhD, Coauthor, *The One Minute Manager*

"*The On-Purpose Person* is the book to read before you read *What Color Is Your Parachute?*"

    —Connee Sullivan, Managing Partner, Tondu Corporation

"I was so excited about *The On-Purpose Person* that I purchased dozens of copies to share with family, friends, business associates, and church members! It works!"

    —Roger Stitt, President, RHS Construction Company

"In my psychiatry practice, I see many patients struggling to find themselves. I help them focus on their assets and get moving—much like *The On-Purpose Person* does. The only difference is that I use psychiatric jargon, attach labels, and charge fees. What Kevin is doing, if it were to become well-known, would put me and other psychiatrists like me out of business."

    —Walter J. Muller, III, M.D., The Group for Psychiatry,
       Psychology, and Social Services

"I read *The On-Purpose Person* with interest and excitement. I kept asking myself: Am I an On-Purpose Person?"

    —The Reverend Dr. Peter Moore, PhD, Author, *Disarming Secular Gods*

"Many books assert that one must have a goal to be happy and successful. *The On-Purpose Person* is the first one to show me how to determine what my life should be."

    —Thomas P. Page, Esquire

"Without a doubt this is the best guide I have seen for creating a meaningful life and plan."

    —Dr. Malcolm E. Hawley, DDS

"*The On-Purpose Person* is a valuable addition to an important and growing literature on effective time management and leadership. McCarthy brings to life and makes operational powerful ideas that will help all of us make a difference."
—John W. Rosenblum, PhD, Dean Emeritus, The Darden School

"The best tool I've seen for turning good intentions into positive actions. Highly recommended for anybody, but especially for those who need a way to organize unstructured time – like clergy!"
—The Right Reverend William Frey,
Dean, Trinity Episcopal School for Ministry, retired

"What's happened to the American Dream? Despite working harder, too many people lack fulfillment, happiness, and emotional security. *The On-Purpose Person* gets us back on track, organized around what really matters, and equipped with a purpose and plan for thriving in a rapidly changing world."
—Dr. Wayne Scott Andersen, D.O., Author, *Dr. A's The Habits of Health*

"Reading *The On-Purpose Person* changed my life. The concepts and practical applications detailed in this wonderfully engaging book empowered me to re-focus my personal and professional goals to achieve true inner peace."
—Gordie Allen, CEO & Professional Sales Trainer, Leads-Plus, Inc.

"Many years ago I had my entire leadership team read *The On-Purpose Person*. The next 11 years we followed and adapted your On-Purpose approach to our specific needs. This incredible experience yielded the strongest management team I have ever had the privilege to lead."
—Andrea Hill, CEO, Hill Management Consulting

"*The On-Purpose Person* is an experience. I read this simple, yet powerful message during a challenging time in my life when I needed actionable direction. It delivered this and more. My reaction was emotional, even spiritual and it has helped me in every aspect of my life since. Being on-purpose, that's where it's at for me!"
—Erik Laver, President, SendOutCards

"*The On-Purpose Person* guided me to look within myself and discover what matters most. This modern parable provides an uncomplicated, yet introspective process. I've shared this message with friends and colleagues to help them articulate their purpose, vision, mission, and values. This small book is large in its power to create personal breakthroughs. The message is timeless and is transforming lives and generations to come."
—Dave Zerfoss, President, Husqvarna Products, Inc.

"If I were stranded on a deserted island and could only have five books with me, I would want three of them to be the *Bible*, *The Book of Common Prayer,* and *The On-Purpose Person.*"
—The Rev. Anthony P. Clark, Dean, Cathedral Church of St. Luke

The

ON·PURPOSE®

Person

Making Your Life
Make Sense

KEVIN W. McCARTHY

ON·PURPOSE®
publishing

Published and distributed by On-Purpose Publishing
PO Box 1568 Winter Park, FL 32790
(407) 657-6000, www.on-purpose.com

For ordering information or special discounts for bulk purchases, please contact: On-Purpose Partners LLC, PO Box 1568, Winter Park, FL 32790

Composition by Greenleaf Book Group LLC

Cover design by Lisa Woods and Barbara Georgoudiou

Lightswitch design by Barbara Georgoudiou

Jacket cover photo of Kevin McCarthy by Marc Harmon

Library of Congress Catalog Card Number: 2007934494

ISBN: 978-0-9740525-5-7

Part of the TreeNeutral™ program that offsets the number of trees consumed in printing this book by taking proactive steps such as planting trees in direct proportion to the number of trees used. www.treeneutral.com

12 11 10 09 08   10 9 8 7 6 5 4 3 2 1

Original edition published by Navpress Publishing Group 1992

To my son,
Charles Claiborne McCarthy,
who was born during the writing of the original book
on February 21, 1991.
After years of infertility-related issues
and wanting to share our lives with a child,
Judith and I were blessed by his arrival—
a miracle even by today's medical standards.

To my daughter,
Anne Guion McCarthy,
who was born on March 6, 1993,
after the release of the original book.
Her arrival was a miraculous gift and continued blessing.

CONTENTS

How to Maximize Your Benefit from This Book

The following suggestions are offered to enhance your personal development and learning, and to increase the value and enjoyment of your reading experience.

1. Read *The On-Purpose Person* cover to cover. Enjoy the story—it's thought provoking and reads quickly. You'll receive great tips to get you on your way to becoming an On-Purpose Person. In other words, get the big picture, then go work the On-Purpose® Process. If you need extra help, we have self-directed study materials and coaching available.

2. As you're reading, if you're anxious to get started, you may want to keep a journal of your impressions, thoughts, and insights. Do what works best for you.

3. Keep *The On-Purpose Person* handy for spontaneous review. Some readers keep it in their briefcase or purse and pull it out to read for highly effective and efficient on-purpose minutes while waiting in line at the bank or grocery store, for their next appointment, for their food to arrive, until the bus comes, and so on. Also, you'll find it helpful to keep it close by for easy reference.

4. Remember this message and the book. Leave it on your desk or nightstand as a visual reminder to be on-purpose. There will be a time

in your life—perhaps it's now—when you will invest time to really work the On-Purpose® Process. When you do, read each chapter and follow the steps. It is all there for you, but remember extra help and resources are available at our website www.on-purpose.com. Go it alone only if that suits you.

5. Each year, reread *The On-Purpose Person*. It may be the end of the year or your birthday. Just read it! Because it is a modern parable, each reading will reveal fresh insights you missed or just weren't prepared to glean in previous readings.

6. Being an On-Purpose Person is like learning any skill—repetition builds proficiency. There are no "right" answers. Move at a comfortable pace. Experience it the first time, and allow your proficiency to improve with practice and repetition. Your happiness, success, and achievements will soar as you learn to be an On-Purpose Person.

7. Encourage others to read the book and join you. Share the On-Purpose® experience. As you grow your circle of on-purpose partners, you're transforming your environment to your benefit.

Read on and have fun . . . On-Purpose!

Be On-Purpose!

Kevin W. McCarthy

P.S. As *The On-Purpose Person* touches your life, please tell me your story. That is a gift you can share with me. Your comments and suggestions are most welcome. My contact information is listed with the On-Purpose® Resources at the back of this book.

DISCOVERY

A purpose is . . . on-going and
gives meaning to our lives. . . .
When people have a purpose
in life, they enjoy everything
they do more!

People go on chasing goals
to prove something that doesn't
have to be proved . . . that they're
already worthwhile.

"The fastest way to achieve
goals," the successful
salesperson said, "is to stay
on purpose."

—Spencer Johnson, MD, and Larry Wilson
The One-Minute $alesperson

CHAPTER 1

"Success"

The mass of men lead lives
of quiet desperation.

—Henry David Thoreau (1817–1862)

ONCE THERE WAS a very successful person.

In fact, he was more than successful: his life had meaning and purpose. He was investing his time on earth wisely and making a significant difference in other people's lives. He had come to terms with himself; he knew his strengths and managed around his weaknesses. Every day was a fresh opportunity to become a better person. He understood, appreciated, and loved many people. In turn, people were attracted to him—whether family, friends, business associates, or casual acquaintances.

But it hadn't always been that way.

• • •

He carried memories of frustration from years when his life had no foundation or purpose. Then, "living" was just going through the motions, stretched out along a string of days spent reacting to circumstances and people. Flashes of clarity were too often blurred by urgencies. There was no true focus or sense of knowing who he really was. He was not in control of his life and not his own person.

That was many years ago. Things were different now. He had learned a great deal since then and had put it into practice. He had learned to be on-purpose.

LEARNING TO PERFORM

As a boy, he felt ordinary, just ordinary. He was often awkward and embarrassed, but mostly just unnoticed. In middle school and high school, he overcame his awkwardness by blending in with friends. Going along with the crowd was easier and more acceptable than standing out. He kept out of real trouble and stayed on good terms with most people. All in all, life was pretty good then, at home and at school.

As a college student, he believed he could change the world, but the day-to-day pressures for grades overpowered his dreams. He honed his ability to sense what others wanted. He knew that the majority rules in a democracy, so becoming part of the majority was a way to gain acceptance. It was an easy, low-conflict approach: Just wait and see, and then do as others do.

His strategy of accommodation worked. He was popular and became a student government leader. It was a rush to have a taste of "Big Man on Campus" status.

Success followed relatively easily. He figured out what others wanted and then acted accordingly. Socializing helped him keep up on the majority opinion, so he continued to be popularly positioned among the student body, faculty, and school administration alike. He had the titles and roles of leadership, but not the heart of a leader. This double life, nevertheless, had its benefits.

He had discovered the secret to success.

Or had he?

CLIMBING THE LADDER

He was in his senior year. College life had been great. True, his grades had slipped, as he could have been a better student. His girlfriend grew more demanding. His relationship with his parents was strained. And his brother was a nuisance. So what? He could deal with all that later when he had more time. After all, he was accomplished at smoothing things over, putting off conflict until another day.

He graduated and took his choice of several job offers. He got on board with a large, well-respected company. His friends were getting married, so he and his girlfriend tied the knot. It was time, and it was also a good move for his career.

At work, he was promoted to manager. He bought a new car and a nice house in the suburbs. He and his wife were expecting a child. His star was on the rise.

Each rung of his climb on the corporate ladder to power and responsibility was hard-won. His ability to detect and deliver on other people's expectations was now masterful. His boss continued giving him good reviews and raises, and he was popular with those who reported to him.

Things were going well on other fronts, too. His parents were proud of him. His wife and children were well cared for. The family moved into a bigger house in a nicer, more expensive neighborhood. His kids began attending a private school. To make more business contacts, he became an active volunteer for several not-for-profit organizations and even served on the board of a couple of them.

His climb up the ladder was taking him to the top. He had the corporate title, financial rewards, and social standing to show for it.

Success—he had it all.

Or did he?

UNRAVELING REVEALED

Maintaining success was work. Somewhere along the way, the shining star of success began losing its luster.

At work, challenges and opportunities were turning into frustrations and disappointments. He was bored and going through the motions. He couldn't quit his job because his family counted on him as the provider. Worse, his personal finances were out of control. The more money he made, the more he and his family wanted, and the more they spent. There was never enough.

Deep inside he wondered, *Who am I, really? What's become of my dreams? What should I do? Is this all there is to life?* Resentment and impatience toward everything and everybody took root. Afraid he would explode from frustration and blurt things he might later regret, he avoided personal conversations and increasingly withdrew from others in a quiet prison of being without a principled point of view.

He was the image of success on the outside. But on the inside he was slowly dying. He couldn't keep it all together anymore. There just wasn't enough time in the day to do everything he was supposed to do, even though he worked harder and longer. He got up earlier and went to bed later. He was always late to his kids' after-school activities—if he got there at all. His parents grew increasingly dependent on him. Everyone's expectations weighed heavily on him. He hated disappointing people.

The company expected him to be active in the community. He felt caught in the middle when he was asked to head the charity drive at the local civic club. Where was he going to find the time?

Things at home weren't any better. Although he wasn't exactly sure when the shift had taken place, his wife's encouragement had turned into nagging. Her conversation was simply irritating static. He responded by tuning her out as background noise or engaging her in yet another inconclusive argument climaxed by storming out of the room. They talked but had little true communication.

The children—they were growing up so quickly! He hardly knew or even talked with them. When their ears weren't occupied with electronic devices, "family communication" meant battles over grades, arguments about house rules and appearance, endless requests for transportation and money for this, that, and the next newest thing . . .

What's happening to me? he thought. *Where did things go wrong?* He felt stuck in a life that was a "comfortable" lie.

TRYING TO MAKE HIS LIFE MAKE SENSE

He fantasized about restarting his life—a new job, a new town, and a new wife. He would be true to himself this time and not get so overcommitted. Oh, for a fresh start and a simpler life!

Even suicide occurred to him as a way out. But *he* couldn't do that. Everyone expected better from him. He knew it was wrong. *After all,* he thought, *what would God think about suicide?* Then it hit him. *Wait a minute—where is God in the midst of all of this? I'm so abandoned and alone.*

Waves of withdrawn loneliness washed over him. No one understood his situation. How much longer until his façade of success crumbled and exposed his reality of disrepair and despair? Life was unfulfilled, empty, and meaningless—there was no point to it. He was just another busy person, not making a difference and just going through the motions.

How could he get back in touch with what was important to him? He had played his invented life role for so long that he was no longer sure he knew who he really was or what he wanted from life—or what he had to give. Secretly he felt he was letting everyone down, especially himself.

These thoughts increased the pressure all the more. He was running out of time—his balancing act grew too risky, precarious, and difficult to maintain. An ever-so-frayed string held his tightly wound life together. But it wasn't really his life. He was an empty suit—an outer shell of a person who was the picture of success with a hollow core. He was out of control, out of touch with his dreams and his true self.

The state of his inner life overflowed to his outer life. He was visibly overweight, frustrated with his job, anxious about his children, and distant from his wife. He escaped by drinking and working more.

In the midst of his "success" he was scared to death and miserably unhappy. His life seemed to be one big snarl of conflicts, leaving him feeling compromised and void. The truth, if exposed, would ruin him.

Attempts to confide his anxieties and fears to a buddy were dusted off with, "Don't worry—you've got it made, man! We should all have your problems."

These well-intended words of "encouragement" left him feeling more alone and confused than ever. He was lost at sea, crying out for help, and the passing boaters waved and kept cruising. Misguided platitudes only heightened his desperation. Reaching out for help was increasingly difficult.

This can't be all there is to life! he cried to himself. *There must be more. Who can I turn to for help? There must be a way out of this dead end, a way to make it work, a way to find meaning and significance. There must be a purpose for my life.*

Something clicked just then. *Purpose.* The word snapped him to attention. He recalled hearing about a remarkable man who was known as an "on-purpose person." Racking his brain to remember he recalled, *Oh, yes . . . he's a college professor.*

The man searched the Web and found the college professor's name and telephone number. Something *had* to change, and he needed help. What did he have to lose?

CHAPTER 2

A Different Path

Darest thou, now O soul,
Walk out with me toward
the unknown region
Where neither ground is
for the feet nor any path
to follow?

—Walt Whitman (1819–1892)

THE COLLEGE PROFESSOR answered the phone on the first ring.

"Hello-o!" answered an enthusiastic and upbeat voice. "What is the purpose of your call?"

"I'm not quite sure why I'm calling," confessed the man. "You're known as an On-Purpose Person, and I thought—well—maybe you could help me."

The Professor warmly welcomed his caller and said, "Please, tell me more."

"I'm considered to be successful," he started. "In fact, quite successful. I'm a fast-tracker. I have a nice house in an upscale neighborhood, two new cars, a couple of kids . . ." His "good guy" speech was rolling—the one he perfected when introducing himself at business meetings, trade shows, and chamber of commerce events.

"So, what"—the Professor strategically paused—"is the purpose of your call? And why did you call me for help if you're so obviously successful?" His tone of voice indicated that the caller had better make his point—soon.

Astutely, the man knew the Professor wasn't buying his well-told untruth. "Actually, I'm not really *that* successful," he admitted. "Sorry. I've been telling that story for so long, I guess I'm beginning to believe it myself. I've been keeping up the charade for years. Frankly, I'm hopelessly confused and my mind is in a swirl. My life feels meaningless and insignificant. I'm so empty, and out of integrity that I've lost the real me."

The Professor listened actively and gave occasional audible acknowledgments to the man. At that moment, the man felt as if he were the only person in the world to the Professor.

"Professor, I'm ready to change, but I don't know where or how to start. Can you help me? May I make an appointment to see you?"

"Your words are familiar," said the Professor. "Sounds to me like you're ready for a different path to travel in life."

"Yes!" the man exhaled.

"Come by my office, tomorrow at three," the Professor offered, "and I'll place you on the path to becoming an On-Purpose Person, but I can't walk it for you. Only you can take each step."

"Thank you, Professor," the man replied. "I'll be there."

Ending his phone call, the man thought, *I wonder what being an On-Purpose Person is all about. It'll be interesting to hear what the Professor has to say. Could he possibly show me the way to a better and more meaningful life?*

CHAPTER 3

The Professor

Enter to grow in wisdom,
Depart to serve better
thy country and thy kind.

—Charles William Eliot (1834–1926)
(Inscription on the 1890 Gate to Harvard Yard)

AMID THE HALLWAY laughter and chatter of students, the man found the open door of the Professor's office and knocked on the doorframe.

A trim man turned in his chair and looked toward him. With a generous wave of his right arm, a flash of engaging eyes, and a big smile, he said, "Welcome! Come in."

The Professor's friendly greeting set the man at ease. Entering the office, the man scanned a wall filled with diplomas and awards. Family pictures adorned the desk, and an athletic bag with several tennis racket grips protruding sat neatly in a corner. Books and papers were stacked in piles on the floor. One award in particular caught his attention. The university presented it to the outstanding faculty member as elected by the students and faculty.

The man's immediate take on the Professor left him thinking, *No wonder he's so respected among the students as well as faculty. This guy exudes sincerity and kindness. He's the real deal.* They shook hands and sat in a small grouping of chairs away from the desk.

They chatted easily, exchanging more bits of background information. After a few minutes the Professor asked, "So, what's the purpose of your visit?"

At this point, the man was at ease with the Professor. Given their prior phone call, he anticipated this question—one of the advantages of being accomplished at knowing and meeting other people's expectations.

"I've thought about that question and our meeting since our telephone call yesterday. The bottom line is that I've lost touch with my true self. My life is accomplished, but meaningless and insignificant. I've invested in personal development seminars, lectures, books, audio and video programs, Web searches, everything. I should be happy. After all, I've achieved a lot. I'm a high earner, I've accumulated savings, and I have a great start on my retirement plan. I'm lucky to have a beautiful wife and two great kids. Most people envy what I have. I'm 'successful,' but I don't feel successful. Something is missing."

The Professor fixed his eyes on the man and nodded in understanding. The man felt truly heard and safe sharing his true feelings with him.

The man continued, "I don't know how to get myself back together again. Facts are–the trappings of success have me trapped. My work serves no real purpose except making money. My marriage is mere coexistence. My family functions like a cluster of strangers living detached, independent lives. I'm lost and alone. Man, I'm hurting. I'm hurting bad—bone-deep."

The Professor leaned forward, touched the man reassuringly on the forearm, and smiled knowingly. He sank back into his stuffed chair, looked the man straight in the eyes, and said with a chuckle,

"Where you are in your life is just perfect! You're actually in a very healthy, albeit, uncomfortable place. You see, we're all On-Purpose Persons—as we say—'in creation'! We're works in progress."

The man was astonished. "What! How can my life be 'just perfect' when I feel so lousy? I come here baring my soul to you, and you—you *laugh!* Obviously, you see something I don't see. So what's the deal with this mysterious On-Purpose Person stuff?"

"I'm not laughing at you," the Professor reassured him. "I have enormous respect for what you just shared and your personal insight. I'm laughing at *myself.* You remind me of the way I was at one time in my life. In fact, it's a typical starting place for many On-Purpose Persons. You're in good company. What I see and what you'll need to learn is to trust the On-Purpose Process. I know what a difference it can make in your life as you progress. Let's talk about you becoming an On-Purpose Person."

The man leaned in to listen.

The Professor pointed to his wall at a poster with a light switch in the middle. "The light switch turned on is the symbol of an On-Purpose Person. It's a reminder that we are either off- or on-purpose— nothing in between. Every time you use a light switch, think to yourself, *Am I off-purpose or am I on-purpose?* And then correct or congratulate yourself accordingly.

"Purpose is the energy of your spirit," the Professor went on. "Discover your purpose, be on-purpose, and the significance and meaning of your life will shine like a bulb connected to the power source."

"C'mon, Professor," the man retorted. "That's easier said than done. Life isn't as simple as flipping a switch."

"Yes, it *is* that simple. You're wired to shine. We all are. Living it out," the Professor said, smiling, "now, that's the challenging part.

Being on-purpose requires commitment and effort, but it creates freedom and opportunity. Sliding through life unfocused leaves you caught between chaos and confusion. Despite your 'success,' isn't that where you find yourself today— off-purpose?"

The truth stung. Outer success was unsatisfying in the core of his being. The emptiness of his life was self-evident.

He thought about a guy at work. When problems arose, this guy's pattern was to withdraw, gather himself to defend turf, and then lash out angrily. *Are we both facing the same challenge, but just reacting differently? A sense of meaninglessness can make a person bitter and battle ready. I pour myself into workaholic behaviors. We're not much different.* A sense of compassion for his peer arose in him.

"Professor," the man asked, "what *is* my purpose?"

"Oh!" laughed the Professor again. "There you go, looking for people like me to define your purpose. That won't work! Others can ask you clarifying questions and provide feedback so you can better understand yourself. But it is 100 percent your responsibility to discover your purpose. Anything less is just people-pleasing. That's the pattern that got you here in the first place. My promise is to show you an approach to discovery, not the destination. I haven't said it would be easy."

"OK then, help me get started in the On-Purpose Process."

The Professor smiled in delight, for here was his favorite kind of student—a person deeply motivated to seek his purpose. The Professor could project into the future where the man had no present vision. The man would discover that to live one's purpose or to be on-purpose is where true transformation begins. To know one's purpose is, however, just a point in the process, a threshold to a renewed life that builds upon the past, embraces the present, and leads to the future even into eternity.

"What's in this for you?" the man inquired. "Why do you do this? I'm a total stranger. I tell you my life is good. You blow through my cover in moments. Truth is, my life is in shambles, and I reach out for your help. Yet you seem to enjoy this. Why?"

Now the Professor let out a hearty laugh. *"I exist to serve by professing purpose.* Helping you be an On-Purpose Person is on-purpose for me," he explained. "And I'm at my best and in my strength when I'm professing purpose. You allow my purpose great expression, so in a paradoxical manner, you're actually helping me."

"Really? I'm getting the better of this deal," the man joked. Picking up on the Professor's comment, he said, "there have been times in my life when I've been, in your terms, on-purpose, and I knew it. There are these glimpses of a sense of sheer joy and divine pleasure, regardless of the difficulty or ease of what I was doing. Energy and life flowed because I was in a zone of alignment—like I was a conduit for something greater than I was. It was a peak experience in an upward spiral."

"That's it!" acknowledged the Professor. "We *all* have those experiences throughout our lives. For most folks they're all too infrequent. On-Purpose Persons are more intentional about being true to their design, so everyday life is more vibrant and engaging." The Professor's eyes twinkled. "Our on-purpose grade point average is higher."

The man was getting a taste for being an On-Purpose Person. "Okay, Professor, you've got my attention. Please help me. Tell me how I can become an On-Purpose Person."

The Professor said, "Let's get started."

STEP ONE:
A NEW BEGINNING

CHAPTER 4

Out of Chaos and Confusion

The man without a purpose is
like a ship without a rudder—
waif, a nothing,
a no man.
Have a purpose in life, and, having it,
throw such strength of mind
and muscle into your work
as God has given you.

—*Thomas Carlyle (1795–1881)*

THE PROFESSOR BEGAN, "Let me print something for you." He tapped on his computer keyboard and his printer shortly produced eight sheets of paper. He handed a pen and the papers to the man.

"While I'm going through my database," he said, "take a look at these sheets. They will constitute your 'want lists.' Each sheet represents an aspect of life. On-Purpose Persons call these aspects our 'life accounts.' Write your name on each want list page."

Heading each page was one of eight life account titles:

- Financial/Material
- Vocational/Career/Work
- Social/Community
- Family
- Physical/Health/Recreational
- Mental/Intellectual/Emotional
- Spiritual
- Other (e.g., finding a mate, starting a business, new project)

As the man wrote, the Professor continued working at his keyboard. The man announced, "I'm done. My name is on each want list."

"Good," replied the Professor. His printer produced another sheet of paper that he handed to the man. "Here's a numbered list of names and cell phone numbers. Call each person in the order as numbered and make an appointment to visit. I'll text them to expect your call. These are your companions for your on-purpose adventure. Carry your want lists and the other papers you'll accumulate with you to each meeting. Get a file folder and mark it, 'On-Purpose Person Folder.'

"Listen to these On-Purpose Persons, follow their instructions, and keep an open mind and a positive spirit about becoming an On-Purpose Person. I'm the last name on the list, so we'll reconvene. I'll check in with you from time to time. This orientation to the On-Purpose Process will set a foundation for your life."

The Professor put an arm around the man's shoulders and walked him to the door. He reinforced his message enthusiastically. "This is the most exciting and important journey of your life. Discovering your purpose is important, but living out your purpose—being on-purpose—will surprise and transform your life for good. See it through. It's challenging to think about life in new ways and perspectives. Expect to face fears, uncover old pains, and push your comfort zone. Also, expect breakthroughs, insights, and a sense of calm. Along the way, your purpose will fill that hole in your soul and bring clarity, direction, and peace. Onward!"

He had met his first On-Purpose Person. The man shook the Professor's hand and thanked him. Armed with eight want lists and the names and phone numbers, he strode through the Professor's door onto the path of his future.

CHAPTER 5

A Single Step

A journey of a thousand miles
must begin with a single step.

—Lao-tzu (604–531 BC)

HE DIALED THE first number on the Professor's list. Already curious about who would answer, he was even more surprised by her youthful "Hello!"

"Hello," he said as he introduced himself. "The Professor gave me your name and number."

"Yes. I got the Professor's text message to expect your call. I've been looking forward to hearing from you. So, what's the purpose of your call?"

He expected this question might be coming. "I need your help with becoming an On-Purpose Person," he replied.

"Great! Would you like to get together tomorrow morning? It's Saturday, so I don't have classes, and my club soccer match isn't until later in the day."

"Fine," he answered. "Where can we meet?"

"My dad's house around 10:00? We'll both be home then."

"Your dad's house?" He quipped, "How old are you?"

"Old enough to be an On-Purpose Person—in creation, that is. I'm a senior in high school. Next fall, I'm off to college, thanks to others who helped me be an On-Purpose Person. The Professor says you're never too young or too old to start learning and applying the On-Purpose Approach.

"My freshman year," she continued, "I was emotionally lost in all the drama. Hanging out with the wrong crowd and doing whatever they were doing trying to fit in proved to be a mistake! I experimented with drugs a little and drank a lot. My relationship with my parents, who are divorced, was lousy. I was lonely, unsettled, and miserable. I reached out to friends but most were caught up in the same situation. It was a vicious circle."

"So how did you find out about becoming an On-Purpose Person?" the man asked.

"One true friend of mine, Anne, is an On-Purpose Person. We played soccer on the same club team a few years ago. Despite my bad choices, we stayed in touch. Anne introduced me to the Professor and other On-Purpose Persons. Thanks to her encouragement and help, I wrote my purpose—*I exist to serve by redeeming hope.* I created my On-Purpose Plan, and I regularly gather with other On-Purpose Persons for support and encouragement. Having realized how bad my choices had been, I began making better decisions. Being an On-Purpose Person makes a positive difference in my life."

"Thanks for sharing your story," the man responded. "I'm looking forward to meeting you. I'll see you tomorrow morning." He was impressed, but remained skeptical. *What can a teenager teach me?*

• • •

A broad-shouldered man bent over and grabbed a clump of weeds. With one tug, the roots were exposed in an instant. With a flick of his wrist, the weeds flew through the air and landed in a bucket about ten feet away. Raising a fist above his head, he whooped, "Two points."

"Great shot!" the man cheered and clapped.

The large man turned and acknowledged his fan with a hearty laugh, "Thank you! I didn't know I had a rooting section here in the Wide World of Weeds." He stood, removed a leather glove, and shook the man's hand as they exchanged introductions. After a few minutes, the yard worker said, "You must be here to see my daughter. The Professor e-mailed me about you. He said you would be contacting her. Go on up to the front door," he said, pointing. "She's expecting you."

The man rang the doorbell. A girl was visible through the glass door. As she approached, he noticed her youthful, energetic, confident athletic stride. It was hard to believe this together-looking young woman ever had faced such adult problems.

"I see you met my dad," she said as they settled into chairs on the front porch. Her dad waved to her from where he knelt to his work. After a little get-acquainted chatter she asked, "You brought your want list, right?"

"Excuse me—oh, yes—the life account sheets!"

"For now it's your *want list*. You're going to use the life account categories to start refining your wants and needs."

"Oh. OK. Got that."

"Great. Let's get started! It's fun," she said with excitement. "I remember my first want list. I couldn't stop. I just kept on writing. That's the way to do it, though—just keep writing. Pour your heart's desires on the paper."

"Uh, keep writing what? And why do you and the Professor call it a want list?"

"Everybody has wants, needs, and desires," she answered. "Some of them are common to everybody, and some are unique to each of us. We also have problems, pains, and failures. The difference is how we On-Purpose Persons organize our wants and respond to problems. We are intentional about our lives—we have a purpose—and we choose to live in alignment with our purpose, so we're . . . on-purpose.

"Your want list is the first step of the On-Purpose Process to help you create order as you step toward clarity. It's a comprehensive inventory of what you want, broken down into seven primary life accounts and one extra, optional account. The headings are simply prompters, an aid, to stimulate your thinking and cluster like wants together. This is the beginning of the On-Purpose Process, so it's important that you wholeheartedly dig into this step."

"I'm sold. How do I get started?"

"Settle into a place where you won't be interrupted for a while and just write. For each life account, ask yourself, *What do I want?* Then start writing every imaginable want no matter how outrageous or unattainable it seems. Let your wants flow freely. No matter how big or trivial one seems, write it down. Hold back nothing, and keep the stream of wants flowing out of you and onto your want list. Write as long as you can, then put the list down. Pick it up again and again until you've exhausted your thoughts."

She broke into a smile. "It's so much fun to let your imagination flow. Dream! So many people tell you what can't be done; this is a time to write down what can be dreamed, imagined, or accomplished with no limits of time, money, age, or health. Envision the desires of your heart and capture every precious thought and unique goal.

"You're the only one who ever has to see your want list. It's your private property. OK?"

He answered, "Yes. This sounds like fun getting it all on paper. Is it OK to flip from life account to life account as the wants are pouring out?"

"Yes, do what works best for your style to get things on paper from your stream of wants."

"For example, if I want to earn, say, a high six-figure income and own a new black Lexus with a camel interior, then this would go under the heading Financial/Material?"

"Maybe," she answered. "Your income want could be placed on your Vocational/Career/Work want list. There are no hard rules here. Place it once in the life account that makes the most sense to you at the time. Be just as specific with all your wants as you were in describing that car. Why not dream in living color? If it's a *core want*, you'll commit to it. You'll get to core wants later."

"So if I want to lose twenty pounds, I'd put that under"—he flipped through his life accounts—"Physical/Health/Recreational, right?"

"Right!" she said. "Capture your thoughts on paper, fast. Avoid getting too hung up deciding which category to put a want under, just write it down somewhere. Let the ideas flow. Later you can switch it to another life account if you feel that's necessary. Generally, trust your instinct to put it in the right life account initially."

"Is there any way I should lay out my wants, other than with the headings for each account?"

"Oh, thanks for reminding me! There's a pattern to use as you enter your wants in each account. Alternate writing your wants between the top and the bottom of the page. As your account fills up, your wants will converge at the middle of the page. Later on this is helpful."

"In other words, I place the first want at the top of my page, the second one at the bottom of the page. The third want is at the top, right below the first want. The fourth want is at the bottom of the page, above the second want . . . top, bottom—top, bottom."

"That's right!" she nodded. "Either that or put them randomly on the paper. One thought leads to another and this is a way to separate them from one another. Any more questions?"

"And if I run out of space under a heading, may I use more paper?" he asked.

"Yes—bravo!" she cheered. "I like your style. Remember, every want qualifies. It's the process that's important, not the rules, per se. Keep your mind running and your pen moving," she added.

"Wow! This is fun," the man exclaimed, "because it will definitely get me back in touch with my dreams and what I want out of life. I can't wait to get started!"

He paused and asked, "So what's the next step?"

"Good try, but not so fast," she teasingly scolded him, wagging her index finger. "One step at a time. Trust the process. It takes some thinking, but it's fun. What you write today will eventually unfold into a plan of action for your life."

She concluded, "When you've exhausted writing your wants, call the next person on the Professor's list."

He admitted, "I wish I had known about a want list when I was eighteen. Thanks for showing me how to reconnect with my dreams. You've a great future ahead of you," he predicted. "What a joy to meet you!"

"Thank you!" she replied. "I know you, too, will be an On-Purpose Person." Her father joined them as she walked the man to his car, where they all exchanged goodbyes.

The man stopped at a nearby coffee shop to start writing his wants. Over the next days, he returned to the coffee shop, where he found the solitude he needed to complete his want list for each life account.

CHAPTER 6

The Tournaments

Life does not give itself
to one who tries to keep
all its advantages at once.
I have often thought
morality may perhaps consist
solely in the courage
of making a choice.

—André Léon Blum (1872–1950)
On Marriage

THE MAN CONTENTEDLY sipped his coffee and placed his pen across his want list. Done! His heart's desire was emptied on the papers before him—well over two hundred wants filled his pages. Each life account held sixteen or more wants—one category alone filled two sheets of paper! As his teenage mentor predicted, it was a freeing and fun experience.

His second call from the Professor's list was to "B. P. Rose." The name had a familiar ring to it, but he couldn't place it. He dialed the number. After two rings, a woman answered the telephone.

"Hello!"

"Hello! I'm calling for B. P. Rose."

"This is she!"

"Hi! The Professor gave me your name." He was ready this time. "The purpose of my call is to ask you to help me become an On-Purpose Person."

"Absolutely! Tomorrow morning I'm playing tennis at the public courts on Azalea Lane. Come by after I finish, say around eleven?"

"I'll see you then," he said.

He remembered why "B. P. Rose" was a familiar name. She was a tennis champion—a former top-ten player in the world who had been a finalist at Wimbledon and the US Open. Later on in United States Tennis Association age-group competition she became the top-ranked player and reigned as champion nearly every year for over forty years. She had more USTA national championship titles and gold ball trophies than she was years old!

ENTERING THE COMPETITION

A tanned, silver-haired woman with a wide smile extended her hand to greet him. "Hi! My friends call me Betty. Thanks for meeting me here at the courts."

"I arrived early and watched you play. It's remarkable the way you stay in competitive form and condition," he said with genuine admiration.

"Being an On-Purpose Person actually helps me compete better," she stated matter-of-factly. "I'm more focused and free to play the game with abandon. And tennis is one of my core wants. We'll be talking about them."

"Whatever you're doing, it sure seems to be working!" he exclaimed.

"Thank you! Our mutual friend, the Professor, told me you would be calling. Did you bring your want list?"

Clutching a handful of pages, he proudly raised them to his chest and stated, "Definitely! What an experience. I started very fast and seemed to run out of wants. Soon, however, I was uncovering buried treasure—dreams I had forgotten about. Several times I asked myself, *Why did you give up on that dream?*"

"Wonderful," she affirmed.

"What's my next step?" he asked.

"Time to play," she said brightly.

"Hey, wait a minute!" he protested. "I saw you playing. *I* can't play *you*. And besides—I'm not dressed for it, I'm not wearing tennis shoes, I don't have a racket ..."

"Not tennis!" she interrupted, laughing. "I'm talking about those coffee-stained papers you're holding. Every want on your list competes for your resources, time, energy, and talent. You need a simple system for discerning what's really important so you can let go of lesser priorities and commit yourself to what matters most. Finally, the system must be flexible enough to incorporate new challenges and opportunities that come your way every day.

"So we run tournaments," she explained. "Once a year I have a major life tournament. I get away by myself, create a new want list in every life account, and I run my tournaments. This annual event refocuses me on my top priorities. Throughout the year, I run mini-tournaments. You'll see what I mean."

He was game, "How does it work?"

"Start by having a *qualifier* tournament with your wants by life account. That will identify your core wants. The core wants will feed into the *main draw*." Motioning him to follow her, she led him to a large bulletin board mounted in the tennis center. "I'll show you a draw-sheet format."

Pointing to the board, she explained, "This is a blank draw-sheet for a tennis tournament. The paired competition format is used for all kinds of sports—the Super Bowl playoffs, the NCAA basketball tournament. Get the idea?"

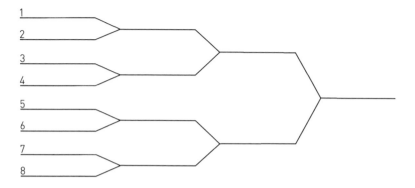

"Sure, I recognize it."

"Take one of your life accounts, sequentially number the wants as they are now on the list. I hope you remembered to alternate writing your wants top to bottom to break up your stream of thinking. In the tournament, we don't want similar wants seated next to each other."

He told her that he had written them down at random, in no particular pattern.

She smiled, "That works, too. Now, number your wants down the page." He followed her instructions.

"Next, create your tournament by placing each want next to its corresponding number on the draw sheet. If you don't have an even number of wants for pairing, simply write the word 'bye' in what would otherwise be an empty slot."

He complied with her instructions.

"Great! Now, look at the first pairing. If you had to choose between want number one and want number two, which would you choose right now as most important to you?"

"I guess, uh, number one."

"Advance number one to the next round by writing it down on the line to the right that's between numbers one and two. Now, choose between wants three and four."

"Number four."

"Okay, put want four on to the next round. If you get to a pairing with a bye, then that want automatically advances to the next round. Continue through the entire tournament, making decisions for each bracket until you get to the most important want in each life account. Each of these is called a *core want.*

"Continue making your choices for pairings in each successive round," Betty encouraged. "Number one versus number four. Which is more important? Write down the winner for the next round."

Something in him objected, "Wait a minute," he broke in. "I just spent days writing out my wants. Now you're telling me to start eliminating them. That doesn't seem right."

She comforted him, "On-Purpose Tournaments are different from tennis tournaments that create winners and losers. All of your wants are winners. Some are just more important than others. Your challenge is to choose the most important want from each pairing and then advance it to the next round until you have a core want in each life account. You are not eliminating wants. Instead, you are advancing wants. It is a subtle but essential distinction."

"Whew! That makes sense."

He continued the tournament until one most important want occupied the last remaining line all the way to the right. As he finished, he said, "Wow, that's amazing clarity."

Betty smiled knowingly, "Take it further," she coached.

"You just ran a tournament with your wants in one life account. You narrowed your selection to one, and only one. How did you make your decisions in each pairing on the tournament?"

"Well," he began, "between one and two, I would give up two in order to get one. Number two was just not as important to me. With three and four, I realized that if I had four, I would have three as well—so I was better off with four. That made the selection easy.

"Finally," he said, "with number one versus number four, I decided that want number four had more meaning to me than want number one, so I selected number four. My other decisions were similar."

"How do you feel," she queried, "about your wants that didn't advance to the next bracket?"

"It was too easy," he admitted. "I'm used to struggling with matters like this." A little light went on inside him. "Hey, this works!" he exclaimed. "From all my competing desires, the most meaningful and important want surfaced!"

"Right!" she confirmed. "And you haven't eliminated the other wants. They remain. They're just lower priorities right now compared to your core want."

"Yes," he agreed. It dawned on him: "I can use this as an everyday organizing tool for my to-do list. Any time I'm confused or perplexed, I could jot down the conflicting wants and use this process to reach clarity about what is really important. It would work on the job or at home for big or little decisions. Writing projects, hiring decisions, restaurant decisions. It would also help with big decisions. When I need to make a sound decision quickly, I can write the wants and then run a tournament. Bingo! I've sorted to what matters most."

"You've got the idea," she declared, cheering him on. "Now, go through your remaining life accounts, want by want, using a tournament to identify the core want for each."

"What if I can't decide between two wants?"

"You have to choose one," she stated. "Choose whichever is most important to you. You'll be a champion On-Purpose Person in no time," she assured him.

Wow! he thought, *that encouragement is from a real champion.* He beamed. "Thank you."

"Get me when you've finished your tournament for each life account. While you're 'playing,' I'll be practicing my serve on court eight over there." She left him to his work.

PROGRESSING TO THE MAIN DRAW

Want by want, pair by pair, round by round, he went through each life account. It was exciting, the outcome often being very different from what he expected. It was challenging at times and required tough decision-making, but he proceeded steadily and finished.

He walked to court eight where Betty was practicing her serve. He watched as she reached deep into the ball hopper for the last tennis ball. She tossed it in the air where it hung momentarily, and with a graceful upward sweep topped by a wrist snap, she struck the ball firmly, placing it in the corner of the service box.

"Ace! Great serve!" he called to her.

She turned and smiled at his compliment.

"I've finished my tournaments," he said. "The results are in!"

"Super," she responded. "Your timing is perfect. Help me pick up these tennis balls while we talk."

"With pleasure," he replied. She smiled in appreciation for his help.

"How many core wants have you identified as most important?" she asked as they headed to the other side of the court.

"Eight. One from each life account."

"Right. These are your *core wants*. Do you know why?"

"Let me try!" he said eagerly. "These eight wants represent the most meaningful or highest priority wants for the various areas in my life. The other wants still exist, but these eight are the most important. By focusing my resources on these, I become an On-Purpose Person."

"Not so fast," she answered. "That's good, but you double faulted on that last point. Wants are not your purpose, just your priorities. You just held the qualifying tournament. Now you have to run the main draw."

"The main draw?" he asked, puzzled.

"What do you think you'll do with the eight core wants?" she asked him.

"Oh-h-h, I see! Run a tournament on the tournament results—the main draw!" he exclaimed.

In the next moment, Betty locked her eyes on his with what could only be described as an athlete's stare, an intense focus on one objective. This shift in demeanor caught him a bit off guard. It was a rare glimpse into the true character and heart of this champion's spirit. She meant business.

"Right. Consider your choices carefully. This is your life we're talking about here, not some game. You'll face hard decisions—five-setters, in men's tennis terms. Once completed, you'll have your *top want*. From hundreds of competing wants, you'll know with certainty the one that is your most important want of all. Knowing your core wants and, especially, your top want will simplify your day-to-day decisions and powerfully advance your heart's desires. The long-term impact of these want lists and tournaments can redirect the path of your life."

As quickly as she made her point, her intensity departed as she grinned and added, "Thanks for helping me pick up the tennis balls. That's the only part I dread about practicing my serve. Yet, it's a necessary part of my being on-purpose. My core wants help me discern my vision of being a champion on and off the court. Being on-purpose clears competing wants and helps me focus and commit my energy on my core wants. On the court, I eventually became the number-one-ranked player in my age group. It's either practice and pick up balls, or lose. No way! Tough work, easy choice! Being a top performer matters."

It was easy to see why Betty was the world's best.

"The Approach and Process of becoming an On-Purpose Person makes a difference," Betty observed. "Being the #1 ranked tennis player, however, is not my #1 want. There's more to my life than competitive tennis. My life is wonderfully aligned and integrated around my purpose, not this great game.

"Tennis plays a significant role, but my identity is not wrapped up in tennis. No, *I exist to serve by inspiring love.* I express my purpose through all my life accounts. For tennis, I intend for my conduct and competitiveness to inspire others to love this great game the way I do. When I play, I want my opponents to experience love." She winked, "That's six–love."

The man chuckled.

"I'll leave you to your main draw," she concluded. "You're a winner!"

He thanked her. He knew he had been in the presence of a special person. A mature On-Purpose Person—somebody who was living on-purpose long-term, with extraordinary success—a true champion who uniquely blended competing and encouraging.

CHAPTER 7

A New Order

Being entirely honest
with oneself is a good exercise.

—Dr. Sigmund Freud (1856–1939)

BETTY WAS RIGHT. The main draw—advancing the core wants from all of his life accounts—had produced some "tough five-set matches." He did it, though.

He couldn't remember having such order and clarity in his life. He had identified his single most important top want—the *number-one want*. Tournaments were a tool for maintaining a steady course—a personal gyroscope amid the chaos. Knowing what truly matters is a powerful position.

He recalled a conversation he had had with his father when he was a teen. His father had said, "Son, if I were forced to make a choice between being a good father to you or being a good businessman, you win."

To the ears of a teenager that sounded very corny, but it stuck with him. *Wow, what a dad!* he thought, with newfound gratitude for his father's loving words. Not every dad said that, let alone acted upon it.

Did he?

A NEW WAY OF LOOKING AT SUCCESS

Core wants serve as a tiebreaker to focus us on the best when the good beckons in all its various forms. His father had made choices based upon personal values. Now *he* was the adult free to choose.

A tiebreaker—what a concept! How many times had he been faced with a dilemma of choices? With a number-one want and other core wants clearly identified, he had a benchmark—a point of reference for comparing his options. Previously, he had made decisions "by the seat of his pants," often based upon a short-term outcome despite the longer-term consequences. "Feeling good" often did not "produce good." A tiebreaker—his core wants—would help him consciously and consistently make better decisions. It only made sense. The more he focused on what was important, the more likely he was to make progress on what really mattered in his life.

It dawned on him that *his own definition of success* had emerged through the On-Purpose Process—a clear identification of his wants and dreams emerged. *So this is what an On-Purpose Person is all about,* he thought.

BUT WAIT . . . THERE'S MORE

Ring . . . ring . . . His cell phone interrupted his musings.

"Hello?" He shook off his reverie to focus on the voice at the other end.

"Hello. This is the Professor."

"Professor, what a pleasant surprise! Thank you so much for all I've learned. It has *really* helped."

"Sounds like you've met with Betty. I'm happy to hear that, and you're welcome. That, however, is not the purpose of my call.

"It's important for you to understand that your core wants are not your purpose," the Professor continued. "Purpose has a larger meaning that touches and integrates all of your life accounts. Your wants provide clues and insights to your purpose, but your tournament results are not your purpose. Many are goals, some are visions, and others are 'to-do's.'"

"OK, Professor. I'm not sure I understand. This seems so right. But, if you're telling me there's more, then I'm your student."

"Great. Remember your phone list. There are more people to visit. You're gaining momentum in the On-Purpose Process. Keep going. Make your next call."

"Yes, sir! Right away. I'll trust the Process, Professor."

I wonder what I'll learn next, he thought. Eagerly, he picked up his list to find the next name to call.

STEP TWO:
THE PLAN

CHAPTER 8

Effective and Efficient

Until you value yourself,
you will not value your time.
Until you value your time,
you will not do anything with it.

—*M. Scott Peck, MD (1936–2005)*
The Road Less Traveled

APPROACHING THE HOUSE of the third person on the Professor's list, the man said to himself, *This On-Purpose Process is fun. I've met some fascinating On-Purpose Persons. Their lives have meaning. Their joy and excitement are grounded in their being comfortable and in touch with their true selves. They're authentic and genuine.*

EFFECTIVE AND EFFICIENT

This house in the suburbs was modest and definitely a home with children. Toys on the front sidewalk and a swing set in the backyard offered clear clues. The neat appearance and well-attended landscaping radiated a pride of ownership and the warmth of a home.

Knocking on the door, he eagerly anticipated meeting yet another new friend—another one of these On-Purpose Persons.

A trim woman in her thirties, wearing jeans and a sweatshirt, answered his knock. "Come in!" she said as she opened the door. "Let me introduce you to my neighbor Julie." All exchanged greetings.

"Julie's an On-Purpose Person, too. Every week we gather to share our progress with being on-purpose. I invited her here to meet you. She's helping me with some baking today." They all moved to the kitchen, where Julie went about her pastry preparations while watching and listening to the conversation between them.

"Please, have a seat," the woman said, gesturing toward a chair at her kitchen table.

"Thank you for inviting me into your home. I see you have kids!" the man said, glancing around the kitchen.

She laughed at the toys about the floor, "A daughter and a son," she answered. "They're napping—I hope. I understand you're well on your way to becoming an On-Purpose Person."

"That's right," he boasted. "I'm in creation. My core wants and my top want are written. Armed with this clarity, I'm ready to work on them. The Professor called and reminded me to stay on-purpose, saying something about a bigger picture, so here I am."

"Oh! Your eagerness to start is natural. What's your plan?"

"My plan? I guess I'll start with my top want and work on it as long as I can, then go on to the next core want, and so forth. That's the way I learned to work through a list."

She smiled and asked, "Do you think that approach is practical, effective, and efficient?"

"I know it's efficient," he answered, "and I assume it will be effective because then I'll be working on my core wants. Anyway, what's the difference?"

"I wasn't always a stay-at-home mom. When I worked in the corporate world, I read a lot of books by Peter Drucker, the management expert. He said, 'Efficiency is doing things right; effectiveness is doing the right things.' On-Purpose Persons do things efficiently *and* effectively. That way, we have ample margin for the inevitable times when we're caught off-purpose."

She continued, "Mastery of time and events is one of the attributes of an On-Purpose Person. We endeavor to do the right things and to do things right."

"So when I'm on-purpose I'm to be effective?" he asked.

"That's right!" she affirmed. "And when you are on-purpose . . ."

"I need to be efficient!" he finished her sentence.

She smiled. "You've got it!"

"That's great in theory," he commented, "but my day is filled with interruptions that knock me off-purpose. Sometimes I start my day with three tasks—only three! Yet, somehow I get off on a tangent. How can I stop the distractions?"

She laughed. "As a mother of two little ones, I know about interruptions. I managed a divisional team in the workforce so I relate to your situation.

"From one perspective, interruptions are disruptive. With an on-purpose perspective, however, my children's 'interruptions' are consistent with my mission of motherhood. My tiebreaker guides me. 'Interruptions' become opportunities to be on-purpose with a quick shift in focus. My core wants also help me arrange my priorities whether at home or on the job.

"To answer your question, though," she went on, "first, it's critical to be aware of being on-purpose or off-purpose. That's why On-Purpose Persons have the *light switch* as an anchoring device. Every time I use the light switch, it reminds me to check whether I'm off- or on-purpose. By assessing myself, I discover room for improvement. In baseball terms, I'm striving to improve my *batting average*—the percentage of the time I'm on-purpose.

"We're all On-Purpose Persons in creation. At times my actions are aligned with my purpose; other times they're not," she explained. "I weigh my actions and thoughts for a day and compare them to my core wants and purpose. By asking what percentage of my day was consistent with my purpose, I can estimate my batting average. It is a wonderful means to monitor myself.

"Being on-purpose requires me to make consistent course corrections with what is most important at the appropriate time. It requires determination, assertiveness, judgment, and honest assessment. My purpose fortifies these qualities. It keeps me focused and less prone to being pulled off-purpose."

The man nodded emphatically as he jotted notes about the batting average concept.

"In keeping my core wants in mind," the woman continued, "I'm more sensitive to changing situations and shifting priorities. For example, my talking with you is on-purpose. If, however, one of my kids starts to cry, my attention shifts immediately to the child—that's on-purpose because my role as a mother takes precedence in that situation.

"Let's get back to your On-Purpose Plan briefly. Here's an interesting idea for you. Take your core wants and run a tournament in reverse. Do this by asking yourself, *What are two things I could be doing to realize this core want?* Keep branching out by twos until you get to SMART actions. SMART is an acronym for Specific, Measurable, Actionable, Recorded, and Time sensitive. Simply, each SMART action is a small step you can do in an hour or less. You make an appointment on your calendar with yourself or the appropriate persons and you act on it. Do this and schedule your next SMART action. Through one action at a time, you'll make consistent progress. For example, our meeting today is a SMART action."

"That's a cool way to develop a plan fast. Thanks for the tip," the man replied.

"You're welcome. It's both effective and efficient," she reminded him.

"Next, let's talk about your Ideal On-Purpose Day—." As if on cue, a child's cry sounded from another room. The woman excused herself to check on her youngster. Julie smiled and continued measuring and blending ingredients into a large bowl.

While waiting for the mother to return from comforting her child, the man pondered how effective and efficient he was. His batting average was low—even by Little League standards.

How could he improve it?

He played with the reverse tournament tip and found that it was an easy way to make a very basic plan of action aligned to his top want. He could generate a number of SMART actions, put them in his calendar, and then work on them one by one. This helped, but he needed more.

CHAPTER 9

The Ideal
On-Purpose Day

For mem'ry has painted
this perfect day
With colors that never fade,
And we find at the end
of a perfect day
The soul of a friend
we've made.

—*Carrie Jacobs Bond (1862–1946)*
American singer and songwriter

THE IDEAL ON-PURPOSE Day the homemaker spoke of earlier was new to him, or at least he hadn't heard any other On-Purpose Person mention it.

Upon her return to the kitchen, he asked, "What about the Ideal On-Purpose Day?"

"If you don't mind," she said, "may I ask you a question first?"

"Sure," he responded.

"How do you feel about your life? Or, in On-Purpose Person terms, are your life accounts where you want them to be?"

His normal response was to jump into his "good guy speech," but he realized the folly of that ruse. He admitted, "I'm far too confused, frustrated, and discouraged in general. Conflicts abound. I'm pulled in a thousand different directions like I'm lost in the wilderness and have no bearings. Everyone has an agenda for me. I run around most of the time putting out lots of fires and never really work on the important stuff that requires more thought and reflection. I'm busy doing."

"Do you like being busy?" she asked.

"Yes! In a way I really do. I feel productive at the time. I enjoy being helpful and getting things done. But when I look back over my day, far too often I've dealt with distractions but missed the important stuff."

She asked, "Do you think this has to do with being out of touch with your true wants? Were they buried below the surface of your busyness?"

"Yes! Too often I'm not doing the right things so I'm off-purpose and unproductive," he confessed. "It also seems that when I focus on one aspect of my life, another area suffers and then a crisis arises. I go from crisis to crisis, putting out fires, never really doing what I want.

"I'm definitely not managing my time all that well. My day runs me, instead of me running my day," he realized.

"The Ideal On-Purpose Day really helps bring your core wants to life," she said. "In my roles and responsibilities as a wife, a mother, a volunteer, a Sunday school teacher, and more, my schedule and life are constantly edging toward being out of control.

"When I worked outside the home my time was actually easier to manage. I could go to my job for eight hours a day and focus on work over a prolonged, relatively predictable schedule. I don't have that luxury with two little ones truly dependent upon me in this season of life.

"The Ideal On-Purpose Day didn't change my circumstances. Better, it helped me change my *response* to my circumstances. Now *that's* important!"

"I'm sold. Tell me about the Ideal On-Purpose Day," he responded.

THE TIME BUDGET

"Let's go through the Ideal On-Purpose Day step by step," she began. "The object is to create a time budget, much as you would create a financial budget. Julie and I like to think of it as a recipe where we mix the proper ingredients and portions to create the appropriate baked good." Julie nodded her agreement and smiled.

"May I borrow your notepad," the homemaker asked, "to draw a 24-Hour-Day Time Budget form for you?"

The man consented and she sketched it.

The 24-Hour-Day Time Budget	
Life Account	Hours or %
Financial/Material	
Vocational/Career/Work	
Social/Community	
Family	
Physical/Health/Recreational	
Mental/Intellectual/Emotional	
Spiritual	
Other	

"On the right, allocate time to each life account by hours or by percentage of a day. For example, you might designate eight hours or 33 percent of your time to Vocational/Career/Work."

"Hardly," the man said, "I work very long hours."

"That's the whole point: In a broad sense, are you assigning your time to your core wants and life accounts? Otherwise, you are unwittingly 'stealing' from yourself, your family, or your employer," she advised.

"Create your big-picture time budget. Don't get hung up on details. Allocate your hours until it's right for you. Use the blank form I created on your notepad." She left him to work on his time budget while she began kneading dough.

BUILDING THE IDEAL ON-PURPOSE DAY

The man called out, "I'm finished."

With a triumphant flour-covered fist in the air, she congratulated him, "Great! Now convert your budget into the Ideal On-Purpose Day. Turn to a new page of paper and write 'The Ideal On-Purpose Day' across the top. On the first line, write the time you want to get up and on the last line write the time you want to go to bed. Between these times, fill in the time slots for the remainder of the day in quarter-hour or half-hour increments, whichever works best for you."

Again, he followed her instructions while the two women continued baking.

"Okay, I'm done."

"Based on your time budget—the first page you did—fill in your time slots with the life accounts. Play with it. You may need several tries to get your Ideal On-Purpose Day to sync with your allocations of time and importance."

He fiddled with it. In a few minutes, he again informed her, "Hmmm. I'm finished."

"What do you think you should do next?" she asked.

"Fill my schedule with the things most important to me—my core wants?"

"That's right!" she beamed.

He entered his core wants next to their respective accounts. It made sense to him that if he were to be on-purpose he would have to ensure that his wants had time to come into being.

Finishing, he said, "Do I fill in my SMART actions with their respective time slots now?"

"Yes!" she answered.

This took just a minute or two. "Wow, that's simple. Why didn't I ever do this before?"

Julie and she exchanged a knowing smile. It was fun watching him experience what they, too, had experienced not so long ago.

"The beauty of the On-Purpose Approach is its simplicity. Let's go on. By your response, apparently your Ideal On-Purpose Day makes sense to you."

"It does. Of course, in the real world I could never live up to this—with interruptions, emergencies, etc."

"You're right. It is an *ideal day*, not necessarily a realistic day. Stuff distracts us from the core wants. Being on-purpose requires a diligent watch on our time and activity. Otherwise, we're susceptible to being pulled off-purpose."

"Are we ever!" the man emphatically agreed. "Can I have more than one Ideal On-Purpose Day—perhaps, one for work days, another for weekends, or vacation days?"

"Good point. Yes, but first, create an Ideal On-Purpose Day to gain a sense of rhythm that best paces you daily. Once you have that, then there are all sorts of ways to use this tool. An Ideal On-Purpose Week is a great way to integrate your various wants and realities of life."

"For example?" the man asked.

Julie spoke up, "My husband and I each create our Ideal On-Purpose Vacation Day. Periodically, we give each other a day like this as a gift. It's a neat idea. In essence, we honor each other on those days."

The man smiled. "I like that. I'll do that with my wife."

Julie added, "Our friends plan days like this with their children. They learn a lot about the child in the planning and experiences. There's a closeness of being listened to, heard, and action taken."

The homemaker asked if he had any questions.

"Yes. Do On-Purpose Persons ever relax? It seems that this scheduling could get rather compulsive. Very 'Type A' behavior, if you know what I mean."

His hosts laughed. "Certainly we relax. Time for rest and recreation is essential, so we plan it into our day. How much relaxation time do you have now?"

"Not much, really."

"You see my point then," she said. "The Ideal On-Purpose Day is freeing, not constraining. You'll probably gain relaxation time, rather than lose it. Take care of yourself—otherwise you're off-purpose. A symptom of not enough relaxation is getting sick. Sometimes a cold or the flu forces us to slow down. We hope it doesn't get to the point where we have a heart attack, breakdown, or depression. Our bodies can't be fooled for long."

The man said, "This is very practical. My Ideal On-Purpose Day provides a foundation for building a daily schedule. In essence, if I'm allocating my time to my most important wants on a daily basis, I can't help being more on-purpose and improving my batting average."

Julie, the neighbor, cautioned, "You haven't yet articulated your purpose statement. The want lists, tournaments, and Ideal On-Purpose Day are tools to help you better organize your present life and clear clutter. In a sense you are better positioned to be on-purpose, but you're really not on-purpose until you know your purpose and then live into it."

The on-purpose homemaker agreed. "Julie is right. The Ideal On-Purpose Day, for example, is a powerful concept because it provides a reality check. As strong and satisfying of a tool as it is, it just makes you more productive but not necessarily on-purpose.

"At this stage, however, celebrate your progress. Now when you schedule 26 hours of activity into your 24-hour day, you'll understand why you need stronger and more defined boundaries for self-management. Go for it! You'll be a champion in no time as you raise your batting average."

His face brightened, and he smiled, "Thank you! I think you've shared the On-Purpose Persons' secret family recipe. I don't have any excuses for being half-baked, thanks to you two."

Two good-natured groans acknowledged his attempt at humor.

CHAPTER 10

Truths

If a man does not keep pace
with his companions, perhaps
it is because he hears a different
drummer. Let him step to the
music which he hears, however
measured or far away.

—Henry David Thoreau (1817–1862)

THE MAN ARRIVED early to the restaurant and was seated. His next appointment was with Perry James, a retired business executive now doing freelance consulting and executive coaching. Soon the hostess was heading for his table, leading a silver-haired gentleman dressed in a navy blazer with a red tie, white shirt, and grey pants.

The man stood, extended his hand in greeting, and introduced himself. They shook hands. Perry spoke, "Great to finally meet you."

After brief small talk, they ordered lunch. Rapport developed quickly and their conversation grew more personal. They swapped business stories and life lessons. It was as if they had known one another for years. The man realized that he had far too few "agenda-free" peers with whom he could freely talk and who could relate to his situation.

Perry focused their conversation. "I have a unique perspective about being an On-Purpose Person."

"Which is?" the man inquired.

Perry answered, "It is important to ask the great questions of life. And it is never too soon or too late to answer them. For example, have you ever wondered why you are alive in this time and place in history?"

The man pondered Perry's question. "I always wondered why I was born. Is there a reason why I'm on this planet? Am I some freak of evolutionary slime or is there a grand design? I sense my life has significance and matters, but I don't really have the answer."

Perry noted, "Your questions are of a spiritual nature. Your worldview influences your life experience. Are you a spiritual being having a human experience, seeking a reason for being? Or are you a human being with a spiritual dimension? Is this physical reality all there is? What happens when you die? These questions are seriously relevant to building your life, yet easily ignored if you are just spending time."

"Perry, sometimes, life just doesn't make sense. Yet, I'm here on the planet. That's reason enough, 'cause if I weren't supposed to be here, I guess I wouldn't be. There must be some reason why I exist."

"You need to state that positively," Perry declared. "Your life has inherent meaning and worth, no matter what your condition or situation. You have a unique purpose that's as individual as your fingerprints. Think of it as your spiritual DNA. Now is a great time to seek, understand, articulate, and embrace your spiritual imprint or your purpose."

The man smiled, "There's probably never a bad time for that." Perry's comments challenged him, yet offered hope and strength—a message radically different from the marketing and media hype endlessly bombarding him with his inadequacies. From the clothes he wore, to the car he drove, to the food he ate—it was never good enough or even enough. This optimism about life was a refreshing change.

REDEEMING TIME

Perry spoke, "If we agree that every person has a purpose, then, what holds us back from living into it?"

"Fear, I guess."

"What fear?" pressed Perry.

"Um-m-m, I'm not sure. Could it be . . . finding out I've wasted much of my life to this point?"

Perry smiled, "Could be. People get into their adult years and look back with regrets over the passing years or decades wishing they could make different choices. Regret is a futile practice unless it becomes a motivator for redesigning one's future.

"When you finally articulate your purpose, you'll find that the 'spent' years of your life are redeemed as 'invested' years. They aren't wasted years, but formative years regardless of how you lived them. Now you have a choice. Will you wallow in regret or rise to living into your purpose?"

"When you put it that way, is there really a choice?" joked the man. "But, what if my purpose *has* passed me by?"

"Your purpose isn't a perishable event subject to obsolescence. It is situation-free. It endures into eternity. Vision and mission are subject to change. Your purpose is permanent and ever aspiring to inform your new challenges and circumstances. Continual personal learning is the cornerstone to remaining a viable On-Purpose Person. Expect the *expression* of your purpose to change and mature over time; but the essence of your purpose remains unalterable."

Perry continued, "My unique perspective is my age. Many of my peers view the concept of retirement as a death sentence—a time when society has used them up and no longer needs them. I reject that thinking. My retirement is a highly productive and significant stage of my life. We On-Purpose Persons find our identity and significance in our purpose, not what society or others attribute to us. In my 'retirement,' I've become more of who I am, more highly directed, and I'm living into my calling as never before. My batting average has never been higher."

"That is a unique perspective. I don't intend to wait until I retire to begin living," remarked the man.

"Absolutely. Begin now by actively discovering your purpose and putting words to it. Thereafter, move boldly in alignment with your purpose. Keep learning and giving and you'll be relevant, useful, and on-purpose. This is one simple truth of being an On-Purpose Person."

"Are there other truths, Perry?" the man inquired.

"Yes," Perry replied. "Your want lists and tournaments helped you to discover what is important. Many things will press or feel good or seem important, but weigh them against what truly matters. Focus on the activities that are compellingly aligned with your purpose. Then, do them. Intentionally invest more time in the essential few and avoid the distracting many. It is so easy to get derailed, but why waste time on the nonessentials?" The man nodded his understanding.

Perry added, "Time on earth is a perishable and finite resource. As I age, I realize the days remaining in my life are a precious few. I am a cancer survivor. The cancer was removed and arrested. My life expectancy is normal and I feel truly blessed for these years. My lesson was learned the hard way. Therefore, I'm intentional about my choices, behaviors, and actions. Cutting loose from the fluff enables me to be more on-purpose. *I exist to serve by realizing harmony.*"

"I understand," the man replied. "My attention span and concentration are short, however. I'm so busy, yet so unproductive too often. It frustrates me because my progress isn't what one might call on-purpose."

"How might you better build on the strength of your mental quickness and agility?" Perry questioned.

"Now, there's a different point of view," laughed the man. "Help! I give up. How might I leverage this 'strength'? Because it isn't happening for me!"

"Structure your days using the Ideal On-Purpose Day as the foundation. Take things one at a time. When another matter pops into your mind, jot it down on a running list and process it later. Then give it a time on your calendar, and forget it until its appointed time. Relax knowing you've allotted time to deal with it later."

"That would work! How do I avoid off-purpose activity? I think you called it 'fluff.'"

"One way is to use the On-Purpose Person's symbol—the light switch turned on—as a reminder to be on-purpose. Being off-purpose is inevitable. Being on-purpose isn't about perfection–it is about progress and improving your batting average. Previously, you had no basis or awareness of being off- or on-purpose. Now you have a heightened sensitivity thanks to the personal clarity you've achieved and the standards you've recently set. The Ideal On-Purpose Day and Week boost your time management effort. When you find yourself being off-purpose, stop what you're doing. Get back on-purpose! With an improved internal gyroscope, you'll gravitate more toward being on-purpose minute by minute."

The man rolled his eyes. "Oh, that on-off light switch haunts me. The other evening I came home from work, plunked myself in front of the TV, and started watching cable news. It's my routine. My youngest child was playing alone in our backyard while my wife was fixing dinner. When I pushed the power button on the TV remote control, the light switch came to mind. The thought flashed, *Is this on-purpose? No!* Spending time with my daughter is more on-purpose than watching the news. Too rarely do I meaningfully enter her world; and so we are worlds apart. *Why not join her in the backyard and do what she's doing?* That's what I did. We had a grand time together. I caught a later news cycle when she was doing her homework."

"Terrific," Perry said. "You're seeing the world from a different vantage point, aren't you?"

"Absolutely! Just knowing I have a purpose and the potential to be on-purpose has opened my eyes. I still get caught in busyness. Over time it's costly."

Perry advised him, "Build that family play time into your Ideal On-Purpose Day for working days."

"Good suggestion." The man made a note of it.

SPENDING AND INVESTING

Perry placed his hands together in front of his chin with his fingertips touching his lips as if he were in reflective prayer. With a thoughtful tone and slowed pace, he spoke: "You said something, 'spending time.' That brings up a distinction we need to make. Business people are fond of saying, 'Time is money.' The concept implies that time has value. On-Purpose Persons invest our time rather than spend it."

Perry explained, "Investing is tied to a future return. Spending, however, is present consumption. Why spend time when it can be invested?"

The man understood. "Investing time, especially in on-purpose activity, holds more promise and returns for the future. Spending time is wasting time."

"Yes," Perry affirmed. "There's a tremendous compounding effect with the seconds of our lives. Time accumulates from seconds into minutes, hours, days, weeks, months, and years. An analogy is interest earned or interest paid. When we are on-purpose, we're compounding interest; when we're off-purpose, we're paying interest. The Ideal On-Purpose Day is one device that helps us invest our time wisely. Consider the difference in attitude and effect of time 'spent' with your daughter versus time 'invested' with her."

"I've never given it much thought before," the man replied. "It's a very different attitude. How do I keep up with all this stuff that goes along with being on-purpose? There are want lists, tournaments, Ideal On-Purpose Days . . . it seems so rigid and programmed."

Perry smiled and responded to the man's concern, "These methods and process aren't meant to create a regimented, inflexible, and compulsive lifestyle. On the contrary, used appropriately they stimulate spontaneity, flexibility, and freedom. That's not to say you won't be called to make tough choices, even sacrifices. Being on-purpose is about maturing into our adult responsibilities while maintaining a childlike awe of life. To live off-purpose is tiring and consuming. To live on-purpose is invigorating and renewing. The bottom line is this: Being on-purpose is about investing your time in what's important even in the face of challenges. Your front-end effort and focus pay dividends for life—real returns on your time invested wisely."

Perry asked, "Have you ever felt bankrupt or empty in an aspect of your life?"

"Recently," confessed the man. "That's why I contacted the Professor. My life was frustrating. I'm learning about being on-purpose, but I'm still living on the edge. My marriage is just so-so. I'm stressed and my back now hurts thanks to my inactivity and extra belly weight."

Perry picked up the conversation. "Guard your core wants. Why run a life account near empty when it really can be full? You have the power to choose. For example, regular, moderate exercise helps me stay healthy. Weekly I monitor my exercise time. Even my eating plan is on-purpose so I am living in optimal health.

"When my time investment averages close to my Ideal On-Purpose Day, it is a good week. When I miss the mark on a given day, I know I've missed it—and more importantly, I know by how much and in what part of my life. Armed with insight into my stress, I'm prepared to win the battle to be on-purpose."

"That makes sense," the man agreed. "You mentioned choices. I struggle with making decisions. Doesn't our past dictate our future?"

"Great question! Choice is power. Past decisions can in essence create 'debt' on our time. Being on-purpose, however, can accelerate the debt repayment.

"On-Purpose Persons excel at choosing. Why do we excel?" Perry paused over his rhetorical question. "We have a tool called a tournament that is an apparent goal-setting exercise. In fact, it is also an amazing clarifier of our values. Core wants reflect our values. The tournament process reveals our underlying values. Here we confront our values and decide how well they're working for us. There's insight and strength in articulating our values. They're the hidden codes that program our choices.

"Sharply focused values simplify life and make decisions clearer, easier, and better. The shift from spending your life to investing it is grounded in your worldview plus what you value and act upon. Clarify your values and you clarify your life. Once they're written, it becomes easier to stop spending your time and begin investing your best effort on what really matters."

"Easier said than done," the man remarked.

"Yes. There's good news, however. Your core wants and values provide solid direction and personal standards. Not acting in alignment with your true self will drag on your spirit.

"Slice life into manageable chunks of time and activity. Most of us are too easily distracted. As an executive coach and business advisor for leaders, I press the issue and hold clients accountable for being true to themselves."

"That accountability has to help," the man observed. "I'm so overcommitted and off-purpose I hardly know where to begin."

"You begin by renegotiating relationships, delegating tasks, and outsourcing projects in order to reclaim space and time for yourself.

Shoot straight with the people involved. Ask for their help. Tell them why and what you're doing. Most people will rally with you. Some might breathe a sigh of relief that you're finally letting go."

"It's hard, Perry. This on-purpose ordering and manner of thinking pushes me. Ultimately, I guess, 'the best me' has to rub off on those around me so we're all better off. This transitional time, however, is scary as old patterns are broken and new, not so well defined or understood ones emerge."

THE POINT OF INTEGRATION

The man continued his questioning: "Perry, do On-Purpose Persons ever go off-purpose . . . say, on purpose?"

"No," Perry chuckled. "Why would we? Do we mess up? Absolutely. At least now, we know it. Creating margin for errors and rest is part of being on-purpose. From time to time, you may invest more heavily in one life account while drawing from others. If a major project or issue arises, such as a health matter, then different choices present themselves, so you adjust with trained reflex rather than raw reaction."

The man declared, "This is really going to help me balance my life."

Perry winced at the mention of balance. "It may seem that way. Your 'on-purpose' efforts to date with your life accounts, core wants, tournaments, and Ideal On-Purpose Day have gotten you more organized. You may have a sense of moving toward being balanced . . . but you aren't. Balance is a myth. Forget about it. Instead, integrate your life through your purpose so you're on-purpose. That's the gold standard."

A bit shocked, the man exclaimed, "What? You're the first person who ever told me not to balance my life. What gives with that?"

Perry questioned him, "So how has living a balanced life worked for you so far?"

The man laughed, "Touché! Not very successfully at all. The few times I really had it together were fleeting."

"So, balance, your ideal for success is—I like your word—fleeting. It can't be very satisfying if that's the case. Always driving yet rarely, if ever, arriving isn't the way life is supposed to be. A balanced life is a model designed for the tangible and temporal world of weights and measures. The implication is that our lives are broken into compartments and it remains in pieces that we balance. On-Purpose Persons use the life accounts method as a means to see the whole from different points of view with better clarity and understanding. Balance keeps the parts apart and ultimately that isn't reflective of life. In fact, it is just plain frustrating trying to live into such a fragile ideal."

"True," the man admitted. "What's the alternative?"

"Integrate your life, with your purpose as the point of integration. It reflects a more dynamic reality," offered Perry, "that incorporates immeasurable aspects such as attitude, love, beauty, character, soul, and virtue. These are qualities of the spirit. Admittedly, they're more mysterious and intangible, so a lot of us who tend to be more left-brained and linear in our thinking discount them. That's a mistake. We can put off the spiritual; but it is never put away.

"Integration, therefore, is of a higher order than balance. Here's where," Perry said, pointing to his heart, "your purpose provides a unique point of integration for the practical merger of the spiritual and physical dimensions.

"If purpose is the starting point, then being on-purpose means a lifetime of living out from the integration of the spiritual and physical dimensions. To be on-purpose is a simple, powerful, yet transforming approach for both persons and organizations."

The man respectfully challenged Perry. "In theory, this all sounds good. In the marketplace where I work, it won't fly."

A big smile came across Perry's face and his eyes danced with delight, "The Professor told me about your spunk. I love it. The battle to be on-purpose is countercultural and counterintuitive. The way it is doesn't make it right, healthy, or even productive. Integration through your purpose is constant, flexible, forgiving, and progressive. You can live this successfully right now. So why conform to a false model and broken world when your life can be meaningfully transformed from the inside out immediately?"

The man listened in amazement to thinking so radically different from his. Thoughts burst through his brain. Was this babble or truly fresh water for his thirsting soul? Seeking balance hadn't worked very well. *What did he have to lose by moving in the direction of hope?*

REALIZING HARMONY

This inspiring conversation yielded simple yet profound guideposts. Naturally he would be off-purpose from time to time. Like most people, he tended to default to the path of least resistance. Now he had triggering devices, anchoring techniques, and strategies to navigate daily trials yet advance boldly toward his future.

Today, at last, his ongoing frustrations and uneasiness had a name: being off-purpose. He was spending his time instead of investing it and trying to be balanced rather than integrated. Armed with new insights, a plan, and tools, his defenses were fortified to resist his tendency to drift off-purpose. Living an integrated life requires effort, but with intention, it is attainable.

Perry read the man's eyes. Emerging was a man with greater resolve, excitement, a sense of purpose, and anticipation for living a truer and more engaged life. Distress was giving way to determination. Enough had been said for one day. Perry closed with a reminder: "Set up your next meeting. It is an important next step with my dear friend and client, Bob Scott."

The man appreciated Perry's perspective. The emptiness in his soul was steadily filling. Perry was right—each of us is a spiritual being having a human experience. He was finally tapping into this powerful reserve. Each new encounter with an On-Purpose Person led to a surge of quiet self-confidence.

Would it last? He had tried so many things and failed. Somehow, however, being on-purpose was remarkably different. It had many of the characteristics of a program but was really a lifestyle, a manner of living with high intention and standards. It was a call to a different approach to life . . . to live to the beat of one's unique drum. But one thought kept creeping into his mind, *What is my purpose?*

STEP THREE:
SIMPLIFYING

CHAPTER 11

Who Am I?

I am afraid to show you who I really am,
because if I show you who I really am,
you might not like it—and that's all I got.

—*Sabrina Ward Harrison*
Artist and author

APPROACHING A RED brick building, the man admired the many flowers blooming along the walkway. A simple engraved brass plaque at the building entrance read, "R. D. Scott Company." He turned the doorknob, entered the offices, and stepped onto an exquisitely polished hardwood floor covered with an Oriental rug. *This place is impressive,* he thought.

"You must be Mr. Scott's nine-forty-five appointment," brightly greeted the receptionist. "I'll let Helen, his assistant, know that you're here." After a quick phone call, the receptionist said, "Helen is coming to take you to Mr. Scott's office."

An attractive, trim woman with short hair and well-tailored clothing extended her hand energetically. "Hello, I'm Helen. We spoke to arrange your appointment. I'll show you to Bob's office. He's looking forward to your visit."

They headed down a corridor lined with framed mementos of industry achievements and prizes, community service awards, letters of commendation from customers, and photos of employees. At the end of the hallway a tall, trim man with graying hair framing a boyish face approached them, flashed a friendly smile, and firmly shook the man's hand. "I'm Bob Scott." They exchanged normal pleasantries. "The Professor tells me you're making great progress in your on-purpose orientation."

The man laughed, "Yes. I didn't realize the Professor was grading me. This whole process is an awakening."

Helen returned to her desk just outside Bob's office door. The two men entered Bob's office. Bob invited, "Please, have a seat. Tell me about the On-Purpose Persons you've met so far."

The man briefly recounted his visits and lessons with the Professor, the teen, the tennis player, the homemakers, and the business advisor. He talked about the light switch, the want lists and tournaments, his batting average, the Ideal On-Purpose Day and Week, investing his time instead of spending it, and integrating his life.

Bob listened intently. When the man finished, he said, "Thanks. That was a refresher course for me. I learn something new from every On-Purpose Person. I love it especially from those of you going through the On-Purpose Process for the first time. Your new perspective and insights inspire and encourage me."

"I'm surprised," said the man. "I imagine you've been an On-Purpose Person for quite a while."

"For fifteen years," Bob answered. "The learning never stops with the On-Purpose lifestyle."

Bob moved to his role within the process. "You've completed the first two steps—*A New Beginning* and *The Plan*. Now it's time to culminate your effort and progress with a workable set of clarifying statements. These statements will help you navigate and position yourself to be more consistently on-purpose in the world out there." He pointed toward the window.

"Great! Let's get started," prompted the man.

WHO AM I?

"This next step," Bob explained, "consists of writing your statements of purpose, vision, missions, and values."

The man cynically interjected, "Oh no! Mission statements, vision statements, and now, purpose statements. They're all the same and pretty much useless as far as I'm concerned. We've done those at work for years, and they just become dust collectors."

Bob observed very matter-of-factly, "That's clarifying."

"How so?" asked the man.

"Your capacity to reach the depth of who you are determines the height to which you might rise."

The man was perplexed. "Huh?"

Bob answered, "Stay with me. You don't know what you don't know. Until you know your purpose, vision, missions, and values and the differences between them, you're muddled and confused at the core of your being. In short, you haven't a clue who you are. One of life's Great Questions is: *Who am I?* A solid answer makes for a solid core. An empty answer makes for a hollow core where everything in your life is adrift and adversely affected."

The man was taken aback by the clinical candor, boldness, and accuracy of Bob's statements. "How can you make such a rapid assessment of me?"

"Please, don't be offended. Core confusion, like yours, is a predictable pattern. Ninety percent of our new team members have it when they start work here. They are great people, but that doesn't mean they know who they are in the most profound sense of the words. It just means they're gifted and accomplished at doing something. We train them in the On-Purpose Approach both personally and professionally.

"If your definitions of purpose, vision, and mission are casual and unclear, then your understanding of yourself reflects that. It's costing you big time. Because you don't know differently, you're skimming the surface of life instead of living in a deep contentment that comes from knowing who you are.

"We've all been there. Beneath the veneer of achievements, title, and lifestyle, there is an aching emptiness of the heart. Accomplishments offer excitement, but soon give way to asking, *Is this all there is to life?*" Bob paused to let this question sink in.

The man grimaced at Bob's words. He had nailed him. "You're right. Accomplishments are like candy that feed my identity, but never sustain me. I'm rarely satisfied."

Bob Scott continued, "This gripping question is more easily ignored than addressed. Instead of going deep, we move to the next problem to solve or goal to reach. We're trained to do, not to be, so we just keep on doing. Defining your purpose, vision, missions, and values begins the process of going within and clarifying one's identity. Here is an unassailable contentment regardless of external success or failure."

With several nods, the man signaled Bob to continue.

"Don't take my comments personally, but do take your predicament personally. Every On-Purpose Person has been where you are. That's why you entered this process. You're paying too high a price for generally wandering through life when you can be meaningfully specific. Confusion leads to misdirection, errors, and waste. This undermines your results and confidence. Eventually, even highly capable people start living in a defensive retreat or taking extraordinary risks trying to make up for 'lost' time. Why all of this senseless pain and suffering just for lack of knowing oneself? Life is tough enough without placing yourself at a strategic disadvantage. Being on-purpose is a better way.

"Your state of being is amplified in your actions. It comes down to a simple choice. In which state of being would you sooner live: confused or crystal clear?"

The man related, "Whew! I'm sold. Show me the way to clarity. I thought I was clear because of my want lists and tournaments. You're telling me there's even greater clarity—a deep inner peacefulness. I'm in!"

THE ON-PURPOSE APPROACH

"As I expected you would be," said Bob. "Let's put meaning to the words: purpose, vision, mission, and values. You'll then write statements for each. Finally, you'll work to align and integrate them through all your life accounts so you are on-purpose.

"Just like you, many people, particularly businesspersons, synonymously toss around the words purpose, vision, mission, and value. Each word, however, has a specific meaning with subtle, yet essential differences. For example, here's a quick one-verb explanation of each. Take note:

- Purpose is *being.*

- Vision is *seeing.*

- Missions are *doing.*

- Values are *choosing.*

"To be on-purpose, we begin with your *being* (purpose). It sparks your *seeing* (vision) which you then put into action or *doing* (mission). This linkage of purpose, vision, and mission is governed by your *choosing* (values) how to think, act, and respond. When your *'being, seeing, doing, and choosing'* are aligned and integrated, then you are *on* your purpose, or being on-purpose. Break the circuit and it is lights out."

"That helps," the man commented.

Bob said, "Let's get you started with writing a statement for each, so you're well on your way to being an on-purpose person."

"Sounds great," agreed the man.

PURPOSE

Bob explained, "Purpose is the bedrock for building your life. Purpose is your spiritual DNA. Each person's purpose sparks and defines the unique essence of who he or she is and distinguishes each individual life from every other."

"How do I write my purpose statement?" asked the man.

"Answer the question: *Why am I here?* It's an easy question to ask, but a demanding one to answer. Here's a hint. Begin your answer with, '*I exist to serve by . . .*' and jot your responses in your notebook. Many thoughts will come to mind, so record them quickly, much like the want list."

"So purpose is about serving others?"

"Yes and no. Think of it as a gift given to you. First, you receive it, next you accept it, and then you can authentically give it. Most of us never really receive and accept our purpose, so life remains an unexamined gift."

Intrigued, the man asked, "So my purpose statement is really long—a full page or more of thoughts?"

Bob clarified, "That's your start. Eventually, you will distill that whole page or pages into a two-word Purpose Statement with the generic beginning of *I exist to serve by . . .* Here are five examples of the purpose statements of people I know: Liberating Greatness, Igniting Joy, Awakening Worth, Extending Grace, and Revealing Truth."

The man smiled, "That's not what I was expecting Purpose Statements to be. They're short."

Bob replied, "And powerful and memorable! Your Purpose Statement captures your spirit in words. Spoken words are creative, and the written word is even more potent. We are spiritual beings, yet most of us are uncomfortable, uninformed, and uneasy with the spiritual life account. Even some of the most faith-filled people are still personally shallow here. Writing your purpose begins the exploration to unravel the mystery of one's spirit."

The man nodded, "This is all new to me. I've never given the spiritual part of my life much thought. I didn't know about purpose, how to define my purpose, or even how to write my purpose."

Bob Scott smiled. "You're learning!"

VISION STATEMENTS

Bob said, "Vision inspires and paints a picture in the mind's eye toward the future. It answers the *where* question—*Where am I going?* If purpose is the spark, then vision is the flame inspiring your imagination, belief, and hope. You *see* your unique contribution to a better world, so you press on during the inevitable challenges because your heart (purpose) and head (vision) are aligned.

"Purpose is reflective, mysterious, and creative. Vision is exciting and inspiring, yet it requires the foundation of purpose. Vision without purpose is a distracting illusion. Build your life on a solid foundation, not shifting sand."

"I understand," the man replied. "You're relating it to the parable of two houses, one built on sand and one built on rock. From the outer appearance, the two houses are identical. Both provide the same day-to-day comfort but one is at greater risk of collapse. The homeowner who invested more to find bedrock has greater peace of mind and structural confidence than the one who cut corners on his foundation."

The man continued, "With purpose anchoring my vision, the structure of my life can be far more secure and capable of withstanding severe tests. If it's true for houses, then it's true for my life, too. When the storms of life arrive, I want my life built on the rock."

"Excellent," declared Bob. "To write a vision statement, use your core wants and tournaments to prime your imagination. You have an image of yourself, so capture the picture in your mind's eye on paper. Use words. Some people actually make drawings. Others cut photos out of magazines. Get a visual and verbal sense of the life you want to live. Do this for each life account. As a result, an overarching vision for your life emerges. This really is a fun step."

MISSION STATEMENTS

"Mission—*doing*—is next. Mission is outer directed and deals with the matter at hand. Missions are specific, external, and action-oriented. A space flight, a newly formed church, and a sortie are each called a mission. Missions get confused with purpose. Because we repeat our missions to become more efficient and effective, we begin identifying ourselves by *what we do* instead of *who we are*. Avoid this natural tendency to interchange your missions for your purpose."

Bob told the man, "You are a human *being*, not a human *doing*."

"Thanks for the reminder," chuckled the man. "I get so busy I forget. What's the question that relates to mission?"

Bob smiled, "It's *What should I do?* Of all of the Great Questions, it is the most popular because it is the most practical. Unfortunately, it is often the wrong question in both circumstance and structure.

"The purpose and vision questions precede the mission question and inform the answer for the mission. If you don't know who you are and where you are going, how can you know what you need to be doing? *Why* and *where* inform *what*. If you live it in reverse, then hope you get lucky."

"Whew! That's a wake-up call," admitted the man.

"The structure of the mission question is best expressed like this: *What do I do to advance my vision that's anchored in my purpose?* Avoid the use of the word 'should.' It implies someone else's approval. It can carry a sense of guilt as well."

The man couldn't resist saying, "I guess On-Purpose Persons don't should on each other."

Bob gave a forgiving laugh and continued his instructions. "Put this question in your notebook for mission: *What do I do to be on-purpose?*"

At this point, Bob rose from his chair and walked to the window. A gardener from the park across the street noticed him and tendered a big friendly wave that Bob returned. "Mission expresses purpose. Mission changes, but purpose is permanent. You've met several On-Purpose Persons already. One is a high school student, a daughter, and a soccer player. Another is a mother, a wife, and a volunteer. Perry is a mentor, husband, father, and cancer survivor. There's our friend the Professor, who is a scholar, teacher, father, and husband. These roles in life or missions are where purpose finds expression while moving toward a vision. Our purpose defines us, our vision directs us, and our missions are when we get off our chairs, take action, and do something meaningful."

Wide-eyed, the man stopped Bob. "I just realized something. I've been living my life backwards trying to find meaning in what I'm doing instead of bringing meaning to my roles. This is a complete reversal! Rather than going through the motions, I can access a deeper meaning and motivation by starting with my purpose. Actors are taught to find the true motivation. This is the same concept, except this is real life, not a stage."

The man confessed, "Lately, I've been going through the motions at work and at home. It's neither fun nor fulfilling. Given this perspective, I much prefer a deep cause and connection than a casual encounter with life."

"Yes," affirmed Bob. "It is a tough shift, and one every On-Purpose Person makes every day. Being on-purpose is a chosen lifestyle.

"Write your mission statements after being informed by your purpose and vision statements. Again, your core wants and tournaments are a rich starting point for articulating your vision, missions, and values. Missions are larger than goals. They're very practical and frankly obvious. For example, one of my missions is that of being a business owner. Keep your mission simple, understandable, and broad."

"Got it," said the man.

VALUES

"Good. Let's get to values." Bob continued, "Values answer the question, *What is important?* You feel your values in your throat and gut, mostly when they are being violated. There's a gag response or a 'turning of the stomach' effect where your body is talking. Much of the time values live in the background and act like guardrails on a highway.

"Values are your ethics and sense of right and wrong. They govern your choices and behavior. Society tends to have *minimum* standards. On-Purpose Persons set *high* standards because our values direct and keep us in alignment with our purpose, vision, and missions.

"Choices reveal the clarity of our values or lack thereof. Everyone has values. The question is whether they are clearly defined or not. Underneath your choices are ingrained patterns of thoughts, feelings, attitudes, and beliefs. As you choose, your values are at work consciously and unconsciously. We can choose to be on-purpose with greater awareness and intention thanks to clearly articulated values."

The man asked, "How do I write my values?"

Bob broke into a smile. "Fortunately, yet again, your want lists and tournaments are a recent storehouse of many life choices. Sort through your paired decisions for insights to your values. You'll definitely see patterns in your decision making. Write out your criteria for how you made decisions. These will be your Values."

"Wow! As Betty taught me at the tennis courts, those want lists and tournaments are much more than goal-setting sheets."

Bob agreed. "You didn't know what to look for in the databank of your heart and head. Now you know the difference between purpose, vision, mission, and values. The more you work with this, the easier the On-Purpose Process becomes."

"Your opening comment about me being confused in life because I'm confused about these concepts is accurate," the man conceded. "I didn't know what I didn't know, so being on-purpose was more a matter of trial and error and instinct than one of a plan and rationale. Now I have the whole package."

"Well said," Bob replied.

Shaking his head, the man added, "Being off-purpose has cost me a lot . . . every day . . . for my lifetime. Yikes!

"Understanding purpose, vision, mission, and values in such a unique and crystal clear manner will simplify and enrich my life. Thanks, Bob!"

CHAPTER 12

Being On-Purpose!

I am still determined to be cheerful and happy, in whatever
situation I may be; for I have also learned from experience
that the greater part of our happiness or misery depends
upon our dispositions, and not upon our circumstances.

—Martha Washington (1731–1802)
First Lady of the United States of America

THE MAN ASKED, "What is your purpose statement?"

Bob answered, "I'll do better than that and give you an overview
of my purpose, vision, missions, and values.

"My purpose is: *I exist to serve by Discovering Treasure.*"

"Stop right there," the man insisted. "'Discovering Treasure' is
your purpose? How adventurous! I like that."

"Discovering my treasure was and remains my greatest struggle.
It is also the greatest joy I can give to others. At one time in my life,
I had a high net worth, but no sense of personal self worth. Treasure,
you might assume, is monetary; that's certainly a part but not the
whole of its implication. Treasure, the way I mostly use it today,
is what's in a person's heart—my heart—that lies buried under a

debris pile of shoulds, coulds, woulds, and can'ts. To discover this treasure is to uncover one's life and therefore one's way in life. It's incalculable wealth."

Smiling now from ear to ear, the man understood why a successful CEO like Bob Scott had time for their visit. He was the beneficiary of Bob being on-purpose. The man jested, "Bob, if anyone needs to have his treasure discovered, I'm your man. Ple-e-ease be on-purpose with me."

Bob laughed at the man's feigned begging. He continued, "My vision is one of being a *Prospector of Buried Treasure*. It is a simple, yet powerful metaphor for my life and work.

"My missions are to dig into the soil and depths of life to:

- Find the undiscovered.
- Rouse the unrealized.
- Redeem the lost.

"My purpose, vision, and missions come to life in my roles as a husband, father, son, employer, business owner, community member, competitive golfer, and church member. For example, at the R. D. Scott Company, we help our team members *discover their treasure on the job*. When people are working in their strengths, their productivity and performance are sure to follow. We do the same for customers. This knack for discovering treasure brings high creativity and value to our customers so they reward us with a growing and profitable business.

"Values guide my decisions. Here are a handful of my values:

- Truth exists. I deal truthfully to the best of my understanding.
- Mental, physical, and emotional health is the platform for my life. My purpose integrates my inner life and my outer life.

- Growth and learning are essential to my everyday improvement.

- My marriage covenant is my most important relationship on earth, even greater than that with my children and parents.

- Work supports my family, not the other way around."

Bob asked, "Do you see how purpose is the bedrock for vision, missions, and values?"

"I get it," the man said. "Rather than having a vague notion about who I am, these core concepts break life into understandable and manageable chunks. The structure is tight with integrity. Can it all really come together for me?"

"Absolutely!" Bob promised, "Awareness alone is a huge step. Consider how far you've come. When this day began, you were fuzzy about purpose, vision, mission, and values as words and concepts. You didn't know that purpose leads to vision which leads to missions, and values provide protective yet life-giving boundaries. Your design and foundation for a more strategic life plan are emerging. Now you're better prepared to be clear at the core of your being so you can write your strategic statements."

BEYOND PURPOSE IS ON-PURPOSE

The man looked thoughtful. "I've been looking for my purpose, but purpose alone is insufficient. It takes purpose, vision, mission, and values—aligned and integrated. Being on-purpose *is* the step beyond knowing my purpose."

Bob leaned toward the man. "Today, your world is that of a life *before* knowing your purpose. Life is good, but it is not great. Otherwise, you wouldn't necessarily be on this journey and we wouldn't be in these chairs talking. We can deny and distract ourselves from who we truly are for only so long. Inevitably, the true self yearns for release. Will we make the journey?

"Your 'before-purpose' life has the 'benefits' of adolescent irresponsibility. Not knowing who you are means there's a built-in excuse for avoiding maturity. It has what looks like freedom and excitement, but it comes at the cost of an unsatisfying emptiness.

"Others go to the other extreme and attempt to control everything. The fear of being exposed, not pleasing, or performing imprisons them in anxiety and micromanagement.

"Either way, a misplaced identity leads to pain and pitfalls. Finally, there comes a point in life where the cost of being off-purpose is too high. Scooting along the surface of life stops working. We want an anchor for stability so our life can make a difference and matter.

"Your want lists and tournaments helped you get the life you know better organized, but it still isn't the life of an On-Purpose Person.

"Today, you're on the verge of your life 'after' knowing your purpose. It will be a different experience. It takes time to transition into being an On-Purpose Person. You're in creation—remember? Core wants are a high reflection of your heart's desire. This focus alone offers you genuine gains and time to reach greater clarity about the Great Questions."

The man recapped the lesson. "OK, by the Great Questions, you mean, *Why am I here?*—the purpose question; *Where am I going with my life?*—the vision question; *What do I need to be doing?*—the mission question; and finally, the values question—*What is truly important?*"

"Yes," Bob confirmed. "Until these questions are answered, we're wandering through the 'before' life. Seeking answers to these questions, however, is to dig into the dirt and riches of your life— to search for the true treasure. Looking within can be daunting. No telling what might be unearthed—fears, disappointments, hurts, anger, unforgiveness, and resentments. There you'll also find hope, dreams, aspirations, strength, courage, virtue, and faith. Most of us are unequipped and untrained to prospect for our purpose. We get frustrated with contemplation and move to activities. Busyness becomes a drug of choice to avoid answering four simple questions that penetrate to the very essence of our life."

Bob warned, "Being on-purpose is a more demanding, yet markedly more fulfilling lifestyle. There's unimaginable power in the personal clarity of knowing and living into one's unique purpose plus vision, mission, and values. Being aligned with your divine design—not the 'you shoulds' imposed by others—is genuinely freeing. Armed with this understanding, you'll know when you're on-purpose or not with the turn of a light switch. This 'after' life holds a depth of personal understanding that's powerfully transforming because of its authenticity."

FROM GOODNESS TO GREATNESS

Bob had an example to share. "There was a woman who lived with the poor and sick. Her income was minimal, and she had no possessions. By much of the world's standard of success, she had little. Could anyone say that Mother Teresa of Calcutta was a woman without a purpose, vision, missions, values, and core wants? Yet that's the woman I just described—an On-Purpose Person with an amazing batting average."

"Hold on there," the man interrupted. "I'm no Mother Teresa."

"Don't misunderstand me," cautioned the businessman. "Phillips Brooks, a nineteenth-century clergyman, wrote in *Purpose and Use of Comfort*, 'Greatness after all, in spite of its name, appears to be not so much a certain size as a certain quality in human lives. It may be present in lives whose range is very small.'"

"In lives whose range is very small," echoed the man. "Wow, that's insightful. I'm reminded of a janitor I knew in my college dorm. He wasn't formally educated, yet that man possessed great kindness and wisdom. To this day, I still draw upon words he spoke to me with quiet candor at a time when my life was in turmoil."

"Career service workers like janitors, gardeners, and housekeepers often can be the most humble, compassionate, and wise people you'll come across. They quietly clean messes and make order out of the chaos and find the joy of serving in what others consider menial labor. Neither status nor position determines their goodness as a person. They bring standing and character to the job, not the other way around. That's why we say, *On-Purpose is the difference in people who make a difference.*

"Every slight improvement in action, attitude, and choices compounds over time. Improving one's batting average, in other words, being more consistently on-purpose, is a solid measure. Being 100 percent on-purpose is impossible; so release the grip of perfection and go for steady improvement year after year. This is the realistically achievable path to Reverend Brooks's 'greatness.'"

The on-purpose businessman continued, "Think of being on-purpose in terms of a percentage of your attitude, actions, and time. Ty Cobb was professional baseball's all-time leading hitter with a lifetime batting average of .366. Nearly five out of every eight at-bats he made an out—a depressing statistic out of the proper context. Comparing his hitting percentage to academic percentages, Cobb would be an utter failure. In baseball, however, he is the greatest hitter of all time.

"Hold high standards and keep a positive appreciation for your accomplishments. Stop dwelling on your weaknesses, focus on your strengths, and your batting average will steadily improve over time. Commitment with perseverance is vital to being an On-Purpose Person."

The man humorously moaned, "My current on-purpose batting average . . . it's a humbling statistic. I'm on-purpose by chance, what with interruptions and responsibilities. It's a relief knowing that being on-purpose is not a 100 percent or even a 50 percent matter. It's relative to where I am today and where I'll be tomorrow. Still, there are people who need me—in fact, count on me. I'm not my own man anymore. I'm committed to so many people and projects."

"No," said Bob, "that's an excuse for not exercising personal leadership. Be more intentional with your time, choices, and commitments. Also, be kind to yourself. Your batting average is meant to help you. Turn it against yourself and your glass is half-empty instead of half-full. That craziness will make anyone feel depressed or inadequate. Focus positively on who you are being, seeing, doing, and choosing.

"Enough talking about it. Take a few minutes to contemplate your statements. Jot your thoughts down on paper. Much like creating your want lists, let your thoughts flow.

"Don't get hung up about perfection. You have ample time to refine your purpose—that's why we say we're On-Purpose Persons *in creation*. In the midst of writing you'll see your vision emerge as well as missions.

"Make yourself comfortable here in my office. Our Chief Financial Officer is expecting me for a meeting. I'll be back in thirty minutes. Invest this time to reflect and write your purpose, vision, mission, and value statements. Remember, begin with, *I exist to serve by* . . . and write what comes from your heart."

IN CREATION

As promised, Bob Scott returned thirty minutes later. The man started, "These are awful. My strategic statements are inadequate, incomplete. They're just—"

"Stop!" Bob commanded sharply, his hand raised palm forward. "You've completed a first draft of your purpose. You probably wrote a page or two. Next, distill it to a paragraph, then a sentence, and finally two words that complete the phrase, *I exist to serve by* . . .

"You've just begun this transitional part of the On-Purpose Process. Celebrate your opening investment in this early step to clarity that can pay dividends in every life account. That's huge!

"Do you realize how few people in the world have written their purpose, vision, missions, and values? Most organizations don't have strategic statements in such robust terms. Practically speaking, it's costing them a bundle in lost productivity, team turnover, growth, and profits. It is costing you on a personal and professional level. Trust the On-Purpose Approach. You'll keep refining your statements as you live with them and grow in your understanding of yourself."

"Thank you. That helps, but right now, I feel unsettled and frustrated that I'm not progressing better," countered the man.

"That's typical," Bob assured him. "This process stirs the muddy bottom of the soul and disturbs the 'comfort' found in being mired in mediocrity. Breaking free of old habits in favor of rearranging your life to be on-purpose takes extra energy and effort. Move boldly in the direction of your purpose and wants. Be expectant and keep exploring. Fresh insights will emerge.

"Now that you've begun writing, you'll regularly turn your statements over in your mind. As this reflection and refinement continues, each will gain depth and significance. That's part of what it means to be in creation. The process is ongoing as our lives develop. As your self-insight grows, expect to revise them. Remember, your purpose is within you. It's there." Bob pointed to the man's heart. "The day will come when your two-word purpose statement rings true to your spirit. You'll know because it will make your life make sense—past, present, and future. 'Click!' In a moment, it all just fits as a whole. Your purpose will hold steady. Your visions and missions will undergo updates, but your purpose will remain the same."

"Thanks for that perspective," said the man.

"Keep an upbeat outlook," reminded Bob. "Admittedly, the On-Purpose Approach initially disturbs one's thinking, but it prepares the way to create order, focus, and clarity so you can build and expand from the solid core of your purpose."

Bob stood again. "Come on—Stretch your legs and take a mental break. You've been sitting too long in that chair. Let me show you around."

CHAPTER 13

The Seasons of Life

We can define "purpose" in several ways.
For one, when we know our purpose, we
have an anchor—a device of the mind
to provide some stability, to keep
the surprises of a creative universe
from tossing us to and fro, from inflicting
constant seasickness on us. Or we can think
of our purpose as being a master nautical
chart marking shoals and rocks, sandbars,
and derelicts, something to guide us
and keep us on course. Perhaps the most
profound thing we can say about being "on
purpose" is that when that is our status,
our condition, and our comfort, we find
our lives have meaning, and when we
are "off purpose," we are confused
about meanings and motives.

—Dudley Lynch and Paul L. Kordis
Strategy of the Dolphin:
Scoring a Win in a Chaotic World

BOB SCOTT GUIDED the man around the R. D. Scott Company. They chatted as they walked. Bob greeted team members and introduced the man. Returning to Bob Scott's office, he said, "Let's get back to our on-purpose conversation."

"Great," replied the man.

Bob noted, "Our natural strengths, gifts, and talents reflect our purpose."

"How so?"

"It is a matter of making right fits—aligning the person and the position. My team members are 'gift-wrapped.' Each person comes with a package of skills, temperament, strengths, and interests—his or her giftedness, if you will. For example, let's take our receptionist, whom you met upon your arrival today. Friendliness is an essential quality for the reception position here. Can we teach or legislate such hospitality? No. Instead, a naturally friendly person is hired for the job because it is part of the gift and strength requirements for the position to be on-purpose. We make sure the person aligns with the position. Even great training can't make the wrong person a right fit."

The man understood. "I'm a businessman; I notice things about companies. Great people work here at the R. D. Scott Company."

"Thank you. It is by design that we're an On-Purpose Business with On-Purpose Persons working here," Bob Scott explained. "We're part of the larger movement of helping every person to be on-purpose."

"Earlier you alluded to helping your employees discover their treasure. That's part of being an On-Purpose Business, too, isn't it?" questioned the man.

"Here it is. We know our purpose and we communicate it clearly and constantly. We hire with that in mind, and we encourage each team member to become an On-Purpose Person through training and ongoing weekly gatherings. Instead of job descriptions, we have on-purpose position descriptions that link purpose and performance and every layer in between. It's a potent and fulfilling linkage when the purpose of the person is aligned with the purpose of the organization. That's called the On-Purpose Principle.

"Each position is structured as if the person running it were the president of his or her own business. That's a concept we call Think Inc. We're all profit-makers. That means ours is a company of presidents, even though I'm the only one with that formal title for the company."

"How do I develop an On-Purpose Business?" asked the man.

Bob smiled and again halted the man with a hand signal. "First, you need to be an On-Purpose Person, so let's hold off the On-Purpose Business conversation for now. We'll talk about that another day. For now, let's focus on you and your purpose, vision, missions, and values."

"You're the boss," said the man.

SEASONS AND CYCLES

Bob turned the discussion back on point. "Seasons and cycles influence us," he began. "As you become more practiced at living on-purpose, you'll become more conscious of the seasons in your life and how to work *with* them rather than *against* them."

"Seasons and cycles in my life? Again I'm not sure I understand. You must think I'm dumb, since I keep asking all these questions."

"On the contrary, you're learning, and learners ask questions. Desire to understand is a positive sign of engagement." The man sat a bit taller in his chair with this compliment.

Bob continued, "In 1962, Pete Seeger recorded the song 'Turn! Turn! Turn!' It was made more famous by the band The Byrds and is based almost verbatim on the third chapter of Ecclesiastes. These words offer a perspective that maybe we don't have as much control in our lives as we think. Go ahead, read it aloud from my Bible."

The man began reading.

To everything there is a season,
A time for every purpose under heaven:
A time to be born,
>And a time to die;
A time to plant,
>And a time to pluck up what is planted;
A time to kill,
>And a time to heal;
A time to break down,
>And a time to build up;
A time to weep,
>And a time to laugh;
A time to mourn,
>And a time to dance;
A time to cast away stones,
>And a time to gather stones;
A time to embrace,
>And a time to refrain from embracing;
A time to gain,
>And a time to lose;
A time to keep,
>And a time to throw away;
A time to tear,
>And a time to sew;
A time to keep silence,
>And a time to speak;
A time to love,
>And a time to hate;
A time of war,
>And a time of peace.
(Ecclesiastes 3:1–8)

Looking up, the man said to Bob, "You mean my mother was right—the world *doesn't* revolve around me?" The men shared another laugh.

Serious again, the man added, "This passage puts life into a larger perspective. Seeing that I'm a small part of an enormous world and a point in the time line of history is humbling.

"Once I was in an earthquake. I felt so helplessly small and keenly aware of my limited control."

Bob smiled and commented, "Good comparison. We On-Purpose Persons appreciate and are curious about the creation and the Creator as well as our purpose relative to both. It's another reason we say we're *in creation.*

"Imagine your life to be like a boat on a river of time. You captain your vessel. Some stretches of the river are smooth and quiet; other parts are turbulent with rapids. Most of the river is an endless converging and mixing of currents and conditions that inevitably move you along. The river exists, but its flow is indifferent to your presence. The harsh reality of 'the real world' inevitably hits us. How we deal with it matters. I've given the responses nicknames: floaters, fighters, fleers, flitters, and navigators.

"Floaters are people who passively resign themselves to accept the river in its present condition. They are co-conspiring 'victims' aimlessly going along for the ride, unwilling to accept responsibility for altering their experience."

"I know the type," the man interjected. "They complain the whole time about how unfair the world is. Why they don't just take charge of their lives is beyond me . . ."

"Now you're describing the fighters. They fight the forces of nature. These people are often high achievers who glory in 'victories' from time to time while touting the virtues of perseverance and commitment. Yet, they fail to realize how little control they possess and how the tides of time wash away their short-lived victories.

Their futile fighting strategy to battle the uncontrollable causes burnout, stress, and exhaustion."

Bob continued the analogy. "Then there are fleers—people who check out of all responsibility and flee the flow of society. These escapees fall into self-indulgent behaviors. Some, such as excessive TV watching or video game playing, seem less immediately harmful. Others are more obviously destructive, such as addictions to alcohol or drugs. The point, the real danger, is that fleers are retreating from society in order to cope with their fear.

"Flitters jump from job to job, person to person, or place to place, always searching but rarely finding what they're looking for in life. They're masters at starting over but rarely take root. Being busy feels productive, but never gaining traction takes its toll over time."

"Aren't we all really floaters, fighters, fleers, or flitters to some degree?" asked the man.

"Yes. To float, fight, flee, or flit needs to be a technique, however, not a way of life. Navigating life and appropriately using these methods is the point." Bob bubbled with animation, using his hands, "Like a mighty river, the flow of time and conditions are beyond our ordinary control. The seasons and cycles, however, are predictable, so we are capable of navigating the circumstances. Even if we 'fail,' our experience grows, and that transforms loss into gain."

The man asked "Does the expression *go with the flow* work in this context?"

"Not exactly," Bob answered. "The approach we take is more proactive: *Know the flow, navigate to go.* We accept the river and its ever-changing conditions. Yet we have not resigned ourselves to futile determinism—we aren't floaters. Nor have we foolishly tried to change nature's course—we aren't fighters, either. We're not running away like the fleers. Nor are we panicked like flitters."

The man asked, "What's the difference, then?"

"The difference," Bob pointed out, "is knowing the river, equipping oneself, and harnessing these resources to work with the flow of water or time. How is your boat equipped? Do you maneuver in the water by using your hands, a paddle, an oar, or an engine? To navigate, do you have river maps, a guide, a GPS, depth finders and charts plus experience, or only the seat of your pants?

"On-Purpose Persons don't have all of the equipment or answers. We make the best of what people, means, methods, and resources are available and seek to upgrade it all and improve as navigators."

"Lifelong learning—that's what it sounds like to me," offered the man.

"Exactly," Bob confirmed. "Each of us owns unique knowledge and life experiences. Add to this our talents, strengths, and gifts and gird it all with purpose, and we gain a powerful and potent combination. When times get tough, we captain ourselves as best we can or we get a more experienced navigator to guide us. This is why so many people today turn to life coaches to help them accelerate their personal growth and professional development. Coaches are like river guides for life. They bring their perspectives and experience to the situation for our benefit.

"On-Purpose Persons know that our lives are meaningfully making a difference. We head into life's challenges anticipating growth, development, and learning rather than defeat and destruction. It is an unassailable position of strength when you know you win no matter the outcome. Apparent failure is full of valuable lessons, just as success inevitably creates new challenges.

"The exploration you've experienced has been in three steps—*A New Beginning, The Plan,* and *Simplifying.* You have gained many advantages to harness the power and potential of your life. You're on your way: Now it's time for a reality check on your destination."

"My destination?" asked the man.

"Your next On-Purpose Person will share that with you." The men left Bob's office. As they walked down the corridor Bob put his hand on the man's shoulder in a gesture of their new friendship. He reassured the man. "This may seem overwhelming right now, but stick to it. Your progress as an On-Purpose Person is remarkable. Oh—remember to make your next appointment. I'm e-mailing John Harold to let him know to expect a call from you."

They shook hands and parted as friends bonded by a journey of discovery as On-Purpose Persons. From the torrents in his life, clarity was emerging. The man knew he had work to do. After all, he was an On-Purpose Person—in creation.

TRANSFORMATION

"It does not matter if you have
been born in a duckyard, if only
you come out of a swan's egg!"

The Ugly Duckling was so happy
and in some way he was glad
that he had experienced so much
hardship and misery; for now he
could fully appreciate his
tremendous luck and the great
beauty that greeted him.

. . . And he rustled his feathers,
held his long neck high,
and with deep emotion he said:
"I never dreamt of so much
happiness, when I was
the Ugly Duckling!"

> *—Hans Christian Andersen (1805–1875)*
> The Ugly Duckling

CHAPTER 14

Choices and Risks

Passion costs me too much
to bestow it on every trifle.

—*Thomas Adams (1633–1670)*
British writer

THE CHURCH CARILLON high above rang a familiar melody that the man remembered from his youth. *Amazing grace, how sweet the sound . . .* Inner warmth brought a smile to his face. Except for a wedding or funeral, he couldn't remember the last time he had stepped inside a church. This next On-Purpose Person—a clergyman—was an unsettling prospect. His thoughts kept gnawing the same bone: *I hope this minister doesn't try to convert or condemn me during this meeting. Church people can be such pious hypocrites.*

Reluctantly, he padded into the church office and asked to see the Reverend John Harold. Down the hallway came an average-sized, solidly built man wearing a brightly colored madras shirt. Drawing nearer, he extended his hand and introduced himself, "Hi, I'm John Harold."

"Oh! Uh, hello," the man stammered. "I was expecting—well, er—well, a minister—at least one with a black shirt and a white collar."

"I am a minister," John replied, his eyes twinkling as a smile spread across his face. "I'm working undercover today. Would you prefer that I change shirts to make it more official?"

They laughed. The man felt a bit more comfortable.

"Please, come to my office." John motioned and the man followed. Yet again, the man was struck by the genuineness, warmth, humor, and settled confidence these On-Purpose Persons shared. Their lives were individually their own; yet their manner had much in common. They were navigating "the river of life" differently from much of the world.

After a short walk in the hallway, they turned right and entered John's office. On one side of the large room was a neatly organized desk with a full wall of built-in bookcases and cabinets behind it. Across the room were several comfortable-looking upholstered chairs and a leather couch.

They sat facing one another in the cluster of stuffed chairs. A framed painting on the wall behind the minister caught the man's eye. It was a simple depiction of Jesus laughing. He had only seen pictures of Christ crucified, or those "sweet Jesus" holy portraits. This painting made Him look very human, real, and approachable. The man eased cautiously into his chair and circumstance.

PUT YOUR PURPOSE TO THE TEST

"So, what's the purpose of your visit?" asked the pastor.

"I need your help to be an On-Purpose Person," he answered. "I'm already a man changed for the better. Bob Scott said you would help me with my 'destination.' How does that work?"

The clergyman grinned and said, "A reality check. That's what I have to offer you."

"A reality check? How so?" he asked.

"It's simple. What's it like being on-purpose?"

"Great! I feel like a very nearsighted person getting a corrective eye procedure. There's a clarity where once there was a blur."

John pressed on. "What difference has being on-purpose made for you?"

"I know myself better. I have a sense of direction. My priorities are in place. That alone is making a huge contribution to my life."

"Let's consider your purpose, vision, missions, and values," the minister said, "and their implications in your spirit."

Uh-oh . . . thought the man, *here comes the conversion routine.* His uneasiness mounted despite the rapport he felt with the minister. He respectfully broached his concern. "Is this when you try to convert me?"

"No!" chuckled the minister. "That's in God's timing. Instead, let's talk about God's design, purpose, and plan for your life."

"Whew! Thanks. Today, we're working on my destination. Remember? Go on, please."

"And so we are," replied the pastor. "Today is a reality check," he repeated. "How bold is your belief in and commitment to your strategic statements?"

"They're still fresh off the press, so to speak. They're coming along. I'm refining them," the man replied.

"My bottom-line question for you is this: Are you willing to lay down your life to realize what you've written?"

"Probably not—uh, not yet, at least."

"Fair enough," John assured him. "You're still getting your orientation. A time will come, however, when your sense of who you are is so strong that you will suffer, even die, rather than compromise the conviction of your purpose. Then you will be richly blessed, for you will have found your true self.

"Being on-purpose, however, can confront and disturb others. It changes the dynamics of relationships in some subtle and not-so-subtle ways. Expect to renegotiate some close relationships.

Your bar is set high. Frankly, being on-purpose can be a tough shift. Some people will openly and actively thwart your progress."

Here was an unanticipated warning about this adventure. The pastor's words surprised the man, yet helped him understand some of the cynical comments and derogatory experiences he was having with other people.

To be on-purpose was transforming everything from his "before purpose" life. His choices were not just life altering for him; they threatened others with change. A life worth living was costing more than he had bargained for in the beginning. To be good was work, but to be great meant taking the risk of standing apart from the crowd. To be on-purpose might be a lonelier experience than he had expected. Until now, he had only considered the benefits, not the fallout.

More thoughts flashed through his mind.

In World War II, Corrie ten Boom's family hid Jews from the Nazis, risking everything for their beliefs. The striking news footage following the September 11, 2001, terrorist attacks on the World Trade Center showed fire and police personnel sprinting toward the struck buildings as others ran for their lives . . . literally. Many risked and lost their lives in service to others. The man thought of his freedom as a citizen of the United States, and the sacrificed lives of those who defend "life, liberty, and the pursuit of happiness."

He thought of a parent's love for a child . . . his love for his children and his willingness to do almost anything for them. Oh, how he had shortchanged them! To be on-purpose may involve "dying" to his present lifestyle. It was scary but making more sense.

Now in a hushed voice, the man asked, "John, the power in being on-purpose is an awesome responsibility, isn't it? My purpose is the very core of my being. Like nuclear power, it is filled with potential and energy, that's much bigger than I am, and touches every part of my life. Without it, I'm empty. With it engaged, I'm called to be a better me."

"Yes, that's right," the minister answered. "It is the power and strength within the heart of your heart. It's your spirit at work."

CHAPTER 15

Passion On-Purpose

It is often simply from want
of the creative spirit
that we do not go to the full
extent of suffering. And the most
terrible reality brings us,
with our suffering,
the joy of a great discovery,
because it merely gives a new
and clear form to what we have
long been ruminating without
suspecting it.

—*Marcel Proust (1871–1922)*
French novelist

THE MAN AND the minister sat silently as the implications of being on-purpose sank into the man's heart and head. A thought the man couldn't get out of his mind was, *Do I have the courage to be on-purpose?*

He broke the silence, "Bad decisions have consumed so much of my life. Is it too late for me?"

"Too late?" John laughed, "You've just begun. Being on-purpose redeems the past and recycles the 'losses' in your life. Your garbage becomes your gold. What you now see as lost time becomes your preparation and equipping for authentic service and contribution. You're in the first stage of a refining process."

"Really?" remarked the man, a bit astonished.

"*Really!* Your purpose puts the past into a new perspective. Your life lessons fall into place like pieces in a jigsaw puzzle. You're actually much wiser today than when you first met the Professor."

"True," the man conceded, "but *wise?*"

"You're building your life on a solid foundation, thanks to the On-Purpose Process. Trust it," the pastor urged.

"I am," the man said. "Thanks."

PASSION

John continued, "Let's talk about the meaning of another word. What does *passion* mean to you?"

Blushing a bit, the man hesitated. "Pastor, can we talk about that at church?"

John nodded his approval, and the man continued. "OK, passion is about love-making, a sensuous and burning desire—even to the point of being a bit crazy. Passion is a highly charged emotional state. Actually passion is something we talk about in business all the time." On somewhat safer ground now, the man declared firmly, "It is a burning desire about whatever one is doing."

"That's accurate but incomplete," John responded. "Let's set aside today's popular usages and review the seldom-referred-to, long-standing definition in the dictionary. It will be both enlightening and important in your present journey."

From the large bookcase behind his desk, the minister removed a dictionary, handed it to the man, and asked him to read the first two definitions of *passion*:

"1a: the sufferings of Christ between the night of the Last Supper and his death. 2 *obs.* SUFFERING …"

The pastor said, "In ordinary speech and writing, the word *passion* no longer means suffering per se, but you'll note that the second and root meaning, although obsolete, is exactly that: suffering."

"Passion means suffering?" exclaimed the man. "That never occurred to me."

John explained, "Passion is a fascinating word because it implies both suffering and joy. Passion and purpose are inextricably entwined. You can't genuinely get one without the other. Like a sword that cuts both ways. Here's the hard reality of being on-purpose—suffering is part of the deal. There's a price to pay, just as there is a cost to being off-purpose. But they're different."

"I never thought about it. Tell me more, John," invited the man.

"I'll illustrate with the life of Jesus at the time of the Passion—the first definition you passed over. Jesus is the true On-Purpose Person. He was willing to die for his purpose. His vision was eternal salvation for all who believed. His missions were to teach his disciples, to proclaim truth, and to go to the cross. In his Passion, he suffered betrayal, denial by his friends, humiliation, beatings, spitting, disappointment, torture, crucifixion, and ultimately a slow, bloody, and painful death. Jesus' life and teachings—as recorded in the Bible and in the historic records of that day—are an excellent study about purpose and passion. I refer you to the New Testament, in the book of Matthew, chapters 26–28. Read this because you'll learn that in Jesus' crucifixion there is also the other side of passion—the resurrection, the joy of going from the darkness into the light by passing through the pain of the cross." The pastor handed the man a new Bible and bookmarked the passage, "This is yours to keep."

The man said, "Thank you. I'll read it. I had no clue that passion meant all this."

John concurred, "Most people don't. Consider coming on Sundays and you'll learn how Jesus can inform and transform your life. He is totally relevant to today's world."

"John, the agenda today was about conversation, not conversion, right?" reminded the man. "Another day, please?" The pastor smiled and with an understanding nod yielded to the planned agenda.

"Admittedly," conceded the man, "I've never heard Jesus described in such real terms before. As promised, I *will* read the chapters you marked. I regularly read biographies of great people to gain insight into their leadership, businesses, and lives. There's no harm in learning more about becoming an On-Purpose Person through Jesus. Why not? Perhaps, as you said, Jesus is relevant to my life and work, too."

The pastor added, "Great! Being on-purpose is likely to mean 'death' of a particular lifestyle or pattern of behavior. Death takes many forms."

The man's core wants were already redefining his life's priorities. The On-Purpose Process was under way. John Harold's tone gave great weight to his last comment.

The man was lost in thought. *Where will this lead? What is to become of my life?* These were disruptive thoughts he entertained. *Change is difficult, scary, and uncertain, but the road I've been on is an unfulfilling life—a slow form of dying daily.*

Despite his concerns, he felt alive, energized, and excited about his future. He was in passion and on-purpose. *What choice do I have? I must choose life—life with a purpose and living on-purpose!*

Standing to leave, the man extended his hand to the pastor—a hollow gesture in contrast to the wisdom this man of the cloth had just shared.

PRAYER

The pastor asked, "Before you go, may I pray with you?" The pastor motioned the man to sit again.

The request startled the man, yet he complied. John placed a chair in front of the man and clasped the man's hands in his. Within this tight circle, John began. He prayed that the man would have the courage to be on-purpose. The pastor prayed for the man's family, his work and calling, and for his life to be blessed in an abundance of loving service.

In his adult life, the man never had heard his name said aloud in a prayer to God. It was weirdly comforting and embarrassing. The fact that the pastor took the time to say a prayer on his behalf was a humbling event.

Upon finishing, Pastor John and the man rose from the chairs and the pastor hugged him. At first, the man's arms hung stiff and awkwardly at his sides. To his own surprise, he cautiously returned the embrace, a genuine sign of mutual affection, acceptance, and esteem.

As an adult, this was the first time he had hugged another man. Oh, how he wished he could hug his father! They didn't express love with physical touch. Here was another opportunity for boldness. The next time he saw his dad he would risk giving him a hug and gauge the reaction. In keeping with his family pattern, he didn't hug his kids often, but he decided to change that, too. Whatever the outcome, he knew it was on-purpose.

Astonishingly, in this new quest, a quiet confidence was emerging. From each On-Purpose Person he met, an authentic connection was made with them and within himself. The On-Purpose Process was making it happen. He was just being obedient to the directions the Professor had given him that first day. Thanks to this transforming adventure, he, too, was becoming an On-Purpose Person.

CHAPTER 16

The On-Purpose Person in Creation

The man who succeeds above
his fellows is the one
who early in life clearly
discerns his object,
and towards that object
habitually directs his powers.
Even genius itself is but fine
observation strengthened by
fixity of purpose. Every man
who observes vigilantly
and resolves steadfastly
grows unconsciously into genius.

—*Edward George Bulwer-Lytton (1803–1873)*
English novelist

A WEEK HAD passed since his visit to see John Harold, "the undercover minister." The man had invested the intervening time to refine what he was learning about being on-purpose. He was eager to reconnect with the Professor.

Sitting once again in a chair at the Professor's office, he was warmed by the Professor's welcome and interest. The Professor began, "Tell me about the results of your many visits since we first met."

"Professor, I have been wonderfully challenged. I'm more focused and directed. I have a profound and growing sense of meaning for my life. This fresh outlook makes everything more worthwhile and fulfilling. I'm confident that as my experience using the On-Purpose Approach increases, true success will follow.

"There aren't necessarily fewer distractions in my life," the man went on, "I'm just managing them differently because I'm more settled within myself. It's easy to retreat into my old ways, especially when I'm around my family. My old off-purpose patterns and ineffective habits remain, but to a lesser degree. If I were a computer, it is like I've got a new operating system and I've re-booted my life."

The Professor laughed. "Please, keep downloading your recent experiences with me."

"The dynamic of my life is shifting. I must admit that this heart work is hard work. Years ago I learned that we train others how to treat us. Considering my old ways, I realize how relatively counterproductive they were. Yet, others seem vested in my not changing. There's learning and retraining happening for everyone around me."

"Yes. Your new perspective makes for a tough shift for everyone. Be on guard with the 'polluted thinking' that seeps into our lives," the Professor warned. "You've begun a good work. Tell a few trusted friends about your growth. Ask them for their support and encouragement."

"Great suggestion, Professor," the man concurred.

The Professor continued, "Other than our choices, we control little. We are born with certain predisposed attributes and gifts, which we can discard or develop. We don't choose our purpose, but we can choose to align with it and build upon it. These 'God givens,' if you will, provide helpful boundaries as well as insights that open doors to opportunity."

"How, Professor?"

"By knowing who you are, where you are headed, what to do, and what's important along the adventure."

"You're talking about our purpose, vision, missions, and values—right, Professor?"

"Absolutely. Gifts, talents, and strengths advance and inform the direction of one's life. You wouldn't expect to grow a tomato from a pumpkin seed—it's a ridiculous thought! The genetics of a pumpkin seed won't allow it to be anything but a pumpkin. Even then it needs good soil, water, sunlight, and nutrients to mature. The tomato has similar needs, but different genetic attributes. Yet, how often do we frustrate ourselves trying to grow into someone we aren't?"

The man added, "That ties into the seasons and cycles of our lives, doesn't it?"

"Yes. The excerpt from the third chapter of Ecclesiastes that Bob Scott shared with you has special meaning for On-Purpose Persons. In the grand scheme of things, we're a small part of creation. Yet, in God's eyes we matter immensely. We're humbly significant."

The Professor continued, "Incredible potential lies dormant within us. An On-Purpose Person accepts personal responsibility for discovering his or her unique abilities and attributes and intentionally engages them in a positive mission. I see students at this college chasing their parents' dreams instead of their own. Other people's expectations may provide useful information, but each of us is responsible for embarking upon the course of our given life."

"I understand, Professor, but how do I know what's right for me?"

"Life is full of clues. Now that you're aware of the On-Purpose Process, keep looking for hints like the seasons of your life. You'll see the signs and read them.

"By fully accepting personal responsibility, you render other people powerless to impose their agendas and expectations on you unless you allow or choose it. Freedom to choose and the pure power of your purpose means your light switch is ON and surging through every life account. Sorting on-purpose opportunities from the off-purpose distractions just got a whole lot easier."

"That's true, Professor. My old way left me empty. My identity was wrapped up in pleasing people, accomplishments, and exterior trappings. I'm relearning who I really am from the inside out. As I accept full responsibility for my choices, will my life be smooth sailing from then on?"

"No. Think about it. Is that what you really want? Resistance with rest builds strength. Constant pressure, however, only wears you down and burns you out. You will rise to face higher challenges armed with new insight and responses, and therefore better decisions. Count on your life being tougher. You're entering life through a narrow gate, rather than walking in an open field. Your on-purpose choices will have some people thinking you're crazy or weird. A few malcontents will take great joy in watching you falter or 'fail.' Others will maliciously and deliberately attempt to pull you off-purpose. Stay in the game. Being on-purpose powers perseverance."

"That's already happening to me," remarked the man, with a flutter of bewilderment in his voice.

The Professor shared a story. "A young businessman I know chose to leave a lucrative business opportunity he deemed off-purpose because his personal ethics were challenged. His business partners didn't appreciate that his values, not profits, were behind his decision. In worldly terms, his decision cost him potentially millions and resulted in a major career change. This gut-wrenching experience sharpened his values and personal convictions. It changed the course of his life and fortified his character. Yet, his purpose and personal integrity are intact and he's at peace with himself. That's invaluable."

The Professor paused to let his words penetrate. "Difficulties are opportunities for On-Purpose Persons to learn and to be strengthened. This point of view is often the only grace or silver lining.

"On-Purpose Persons seek true success in people, relationships, faith, love, and service—not in things. There is nothing wrong with possessions, that is, until the possessions possess us. That's trouble.

"Goals are worthy. Define your standards for success. Some measure success in dollars earned or possessions owned. Others answer a call where success is measured in terms of lives saved, minds taught, people served, and love given."

"Professor," commented the man, "being an On-Purpose Person is tough work. It's counter to our culture. Not being intentional about life is that easygoing, just 'floating down the river,' approach. Whatever happens, happens. On-Purpose Persons, on the other hand, chart an action plan and execute. It's more demanding to be on-purpose—to be a navigator."

"Yes. Being on-purpose is proactive." The Professor noted, "You're coming along nicely. You must be pleased." The man nodded his agreement.

The Professor added, "You still have a couple of steps to go in your orientation."

CHAPTER 17

Giving

We make a living by what
we get, but we make a life
by what we give.

—*Winston Churchill (1874–1965)*

"FIRST, IT'S REVIEW time. What have you learned so far about the On-Purpose Process?" quizzed the Professor.

The man replied, "The method of want lists and tournaments moved me quickly from confusion into crystal clear thinking with more defined action. The Ideal On-Purpose Day has me much more aware and productive. My purpose, vision, missions, and values help me make consistently better and faster decisions.

"This is a confidence-building process. Even this early into being on-purpose, I'm getting more done with less effort because I'm focused on what's important and less distracted. I truly see how I make a significant difference in the world regardless of my situation."

"Wonderful," acknowledged the Professor. "Surely you've heard the others say, 'On-Purpose is the difference in people who make a difference.'"

"Yes," the man replied. "It sounded like double-speak to me the first time I heard it. Now, I appreciate the meaning and intent."

The Professor pushed on. "Let's diagram it. Most people want to make a difference with their lives. Contributing to the well-being of others is ingrained in the human spirit, even in the roughest of characters. Yet, many of us don't have a clue about how to do that or what steps to take. The On-Purpose Process is a simple, powerful way to smoothly and smartly transition from chaos and confusion to clarity and then to true contribution.

"Articulating your purpose is a one-time epiphany. Celebrate that, but it's just the beginning. Being on-purpose or living consistently in alignment with your purpose is the real action. To know your purpose but to park it because of lingering fears, vanity, or insecurity takes a tragic toll on a life. Hoarding yourself atrophies your purpose, talent, strengths, and gifts. Being off-purpose makes for a needlessly diminished life, and the world loses.

"Instead, be bold. Your purpose informs your life, calling, and unique contribution. If every person on the earth knew his or her purpose and was living on-purpose, the world would be a better place."

The man grinned and offered a suggestion. "We could call it The On-Purpose Planet."

"I like it," the Professor said. "Every person on-purpose."

The man said, "Being on-purpose helps me make sense of my life. This insight provides internal accountability and higher personal standards. My constant need for the approval of others produced a counterfeit identity. I didn't know who I was. Now, my sense of myself is growing daily along with a blossoming inner confidence."

The Professor picked up on the man's comments. "Good. Sounds like you're ready for your next lesson in life leadership. Your focus and attention thus far have been rightfully on yourself these many visits, yes?"

"I agree."

The Professor said, "The steps you've taken are a solid foundation. Now it's time to direct your gains to the good of your family, friends, clients, and the community."

GENEROUS GIVING

"Professor," the man broke in, "where do I start? The needs are overwhelming. What do I have to give? Who should I give to? When do I have time to give? What difference can I make?"

"The answer to all your questions is . . ." The Professor paused. "I'll give you a hint: It begins with making a list."

The man picked up immediately on the Professor's clue, "Oh, make a give list like a want list, and then run a tournament to identify my top giving. Of course!"

"Yes, yes," affirmed the Professor. "Giving touches every life account. Again, your purpose is the point of integration. Now your purpose is a key filter for discerning where and to whom to give of yourself. Giving, however, is generally an underdeveloped concept. On-Purpose Persons are joyful, intentional, and proportional givers. All three elements need to be present."

"I'm game, Professor. Why do you say giving is *joyful*?"

"Giving out of joy and thanksgiving for our blessings and abundance are the building blocks for true giving. You've recently had the opportunity for some intense self-discovery. Knowing yourself better means you're more aware of your special gifts and talents that especially qualify you to serve. No one else in the world is exactly like you. Someone or some cause needs you. Think of them as your 'customers' or 'audience' awaiting your performance.

"From this appreciation of yourself, you will naturally share from your strength. Your prior mind-set may have been one of scarcity rather than abundance. Trust your instinct to give with joy."

"Whew, Professor, I hear you. I've worked hard to get what I have and to be where I am in life."

"Of course you have. That's why your first gift is giving 10 percent of your income to those in need. You make your second gift to yourself and your family by saving."

"That's daunting. I'm barely managing my expenses now."

"You're not alone. That's why giving must be *intentional*—in other words, a committed priority."

"How do I fit yet another priority into my life?"

"You don't *fit it*–it is an attitude first; then an action. Life is a wonderful gift. Recognize it as such. Receive and accept it. From the bounty of your appreciation for every breath, you'll want to serve."

"Whoa, Professor. Now there's a radical statement. You mean, I'm to turn my recently ordered on-purpose person life upside down and put aside my core wants? Do you want me to be a third-world missionary or something? It's all made sense until now."

The Professor chuckled as he admired the man's candor, "No and no. Hear me out. Remember I said giving is joyful, intentional, *and* proportional. Let's talk about giving in proportion to our means.

"On-Purpose Persons have a minimum standard of giving," explained the Professor. "We keep as much as 90 percent of what we receive, including the 10 percent that we save. In other words, we give a minimum of 10 percent to others—that's giving in proportion to our means. My resources are different from yours. Our means are different from those of an unemployed person or the CEO of a Fortune 500 company. The only difference is the scale, yet the standard remains the same.

"We measure ourselves in proportional terms, rather than absolute terms. Comparing your giving to another person is an ineffective and defeating exercise. Being on-purpose fosters a realization of abundance, so there's an inherent overflow of appreciation from the heart. A vision emerges in the mind's eye and is followed by a mission of giving. Your values will govern your giving. This is a basic virtue of generous giving."

The Professor added a reassuring aside to the man's earlier question. "By the way, be a third-world missionary only if it is on-purpose."

"That's a relief!" They both smiled.

TIME, TALENT, AND TREASURE

The man continued clarifying. "How do you define our means, Professor?"

"Our means are our time, talent, and treasure."

"How do I give of my time? My Ideal On-Purpose Day is already scheduled and keeps me on-purpose."

"Give first. Remember, you will determine your core giving just like you discovered your core wants. You can only allocate so much time to so many giving opportunities, so select ones that are on-purpose.

"Ten percent of your day translates into two hours and twenty-four minutes of giving. Typically, that won't happen in one big block of time. You may accumulate your giving time over a week and do it all in one day. You can give of your time through volunteer opportunities as well as small spontaneous acts of kindness or courtesy."

"That is a lot of time," the man expressed. "Where am I supposed to find time like that?"

"You integrate it into your daily routine. Create an Ideal On-Purpose Day with giving. You get up, you exercise, you go to work, you come home, you eat, and you go to bed. Pretty basic stuff, wouldn't you say?"

The man nodded his agreement.

"Here are your opportunities to give. When you awaken, hold and hug your wife for two minutes. Tell her you love her as you arise from bed. While on your morning jog, greet neighbors and other runners with a smile or complimentary remark.

"Upon returning home, instead of dumping your sweaty clothes on the floor, put them in the washer along with a load of other clothes. Help one of the kids pack her lunch for school—joyfully. Send a card or handwritten note of appreciation to someone every day.

"When driving to work, let another driver into the line of traffic ahead of you. At work, take five minutes to really listen to your assistant and ten more minutes to help her—joyfully—with something she doesn't understand. Thank an employee, vendor, or customer. At noon, hold the door to the restaurant for an elderly man with a cane who's fifteen seconds behind you and, when he passes by, smile and greet him. If appropriate, place a hand respectfully on his shoulder. People respond to smiles and touch.

"As you leave your office, acknowledge and thank the janitor for cleaning the office and let him know how much you appreciate his work. Wave at another person or two caught in rush hour traffic. Smile at them. Be genuine in your giving."

"Professor, I get the idea. You're right; it's basic courtesy and an awareness of the hundreds, if not thousands, of giving opportunities that present themselves in every day events."

The Professor continued, "It is attitude and awareness in action. Formally structured volunteer opportunities also abound. On-Purpose Persons plan a portion of their giving. For example, the head football coach here at this college is a burly On-Purpose Person and a former NFL all-pro lineman. In the off-season he goes to a local children's hospital to hold, rock, and love on newborn babies—babies who have drug-addicted moms. Some are so small they fit in his gnarled bear paw of a hand. There's a volunteer opportunity for you in your church, civic organization, school, hospital, or not-for-profit organization somewhere in the community."

"I see that. Giving of my talent is easy to figure out, Professor. May I tell you what I think it involves?"

"Yes, go on," said the Professor.

"I'm an accomplished amateur magician. I love it, but I don't have reason or time to practice my tricks. Perhaps I could go to the local children's hospital to entertain the kids or to a retirement center to kibitz with the elderly. It would be fun. In fact, it was on my want list."

"Great idea. Giving opportunities are ways to create win-win situations. Professionals such as doctors, lawyers, accountants, and consultants may give in-kind expertise to nonprofit organizations or needy persons. Giving may be an opportunity to do something totally different from our work—like the football coach. Our talents need not be perfected, just available.

"For example, we can hold someone's hand, so we can comfort at a nursing home or hospital. We can drive a car, so we can deliver food to shut-ins through an organization like Meals on Wheels. We can read, so we can volunteer through Reading Is Fundamental. The Points of Light Foundation connects people to volunteer centers with many needs. The Leukemia & Lymphoma Society conducts running and walking events to fund finding a cure for blood cancers. The opportunities are endless. Search the Internet. You'll find that many great causes need you.

"Now let's talk about treasure," the Professor said, changing the subject a little.

"OK," agreed the man. "Bob Scott talked about treasure."

"That's right. His purpose statement is *Discovering Treasure.*

"Let's focus first on money as treasure. Giving our time and talent is often one thing, but to reach into one's wallet is a different challenge. Let me reaffirm the On-Purpose Person's giving standard: We joyfully and intentionally give away the first 10 percent of our income. This means we keep a maximum of 90 percent of what we earn for saving, investing, or spending."

"You've got be kidding—*10 percent* of what I make goes to others? Off the top? I'm leveraged to the hilt! There's no way," protested the man, shaking his head.

"Think of it as a return on investment for the life you've received. Make giving a priority. In other words, self-worth is not to be wrapped up in the size of a paycheck or house or the kind of car we drive. Material goods disappear as quickly as they appear, so why build a life on that sandy foundation?"

"Professor, I take issue with this," the man asserted respectfully. "It sounds like academic idealism. There's a real world out there I have to live in . . . and it wants the bills paid monthly."

The Professor smiled, rubbed his chin, and sat back in his chair before speaking. "Your directness is refreshing. Let me pose another question: Do your possessions possess you, or do you possess them?"

The man thought aloud, "To some degree, I'm addicted to stuff . . . and more stuff. All the things I've accumulated amount to comfort, not peace. I don't know the answer to your question. Still, giving 10 percent is challenging."

"Figure out what is enough, then wean yourself from your 'stuff,'" advised the Professor. "Otherwise you'll just keep mindlessly accumulating more stuff. For example, could you and your wife develop a household budget and steadily increase your giving?" asked the Professor.

"That's possible. We're probably giving about 2 percent of our income to charities now. If we cut a few luxuries and increased our giving another 2 percent each year for the next four years we might manage to get there," the man conceded.

"Great! There's a plan."

The man volunteered, "After my next annual review, a large part of my raise or bonus could go to giving instead of ramping up our lifestyle. This way we could hit the 10 percent goal even faster."

"Now that is giving done joyfully, intentionally, and in thanksgiving from your abundance," commented the Professor. "You've caught the attitude of gratitude because you're looking for ways to give."

"Professor, it makes sense, but this is a struggle and is going to take some soul-searching."

"Exactly. Cutting free from 'the dark side' of materialism is tough. Give 10 percent and save 10 percent. By creating this much margin in your life, you'll be living well within your earnings and free to give within your means. Giving and saving are two sides of the same principle of not letting money and things rule you. Master your money, and you redeem a big part of your identity.

"Wouldn't it be great if your children grew up free from the attitude that their self-worth directly equated to their net worth? You can help free them from this cultural trap. Make giving a family project. Involve your wife and children in giving projects. Put your time, talent, and treasure into action. It will be an unforgettable lesson for your children."

"What a cool idea for my family to develop character!"

NATURAL TREASURE

The Professor said, "Another aspect of our treasure is our natural resources. In the biggest sense, there's the planet and our environment. In the most personal sense, our natural resources are our intellect and physical bodies.

"Our environment has renewable resources. For example, trees absorb nutrients and light to produce life-giving oxygen; they drop their leaves and create more nutrients, and so goes the cycle.

"We also possess renewable natural resources. Physically, blood and bone marrow can be donated to save a life. There are also natural resources we can impart to one another. An organ donor gives life to others through transplant surgery. They see life beyond themselves in an on-purpose act of giving.

"A smile, a compliment, a hug, and a kiss are also examples of unlimited natural resources. So, be generous."

The man nodded in agreement. "I never noticed how many ways there are to give. Is there a greatest giving of all?"

"Oh, yes! Love is the greatest gift of all," declared the Professor. "It's an unlimited resource. The more you give, the more you receive. This great truth inspires all giving."

"Professor, we *do* depend on one another. Giving is an essential ingredient for living well. The image of the strong loner makes for a good story, but I'll attest that it is a challenging life. The help from the other On-Purpose Persons was hard to accept at first. Call it pride or stupidity, but I've never been willing to expose my needs for fear of appearing weak. It has been lonely and, frankly, very unproductive.

"I don't think I'm alone, either. Lots of people hurt down deep, but they, too, have mastered the self-sufficient façade. I see it in their eyes and on their faces. Stress, overeating, drinking, addiction, affairs, and ill health are slowly killing their bodies. Their spirit died long before. I was well down that road when I called you."

"Sounds like you've got the picture about joyful, intentional, and proportional giving.

"Tomorrow we're scheduled for another meeting. Tonight, create your giving list. Be sure to look at your want list for giving. There's gold there waiting to be mined. Sift through your want lists for giving wants. Add these to your giving list. Run your tournament to advance your core giving, and then re-organize your Ideal On-Purpose Day with giving. Review your purpose, vision, missions, and values for any refinements you want to make. Remember, 'I exist *to serve* by . . .' starts your purpose statement. Serving is giving and brings rich expression to your purpose."

"Whew, I'd better get going. I can't wait to get started on my give list!" exclaimed the man.

"Then get! By the way, instead of meeting in my office tomorrow, let's meet in room 412, the conference room down the hall. Be there at four o'clock."

CHAPTER 18

The Gathering

Union gives strength.

—*Aesop (550 BC)*
"The Bundle of Sticks"

OPENING THE DOOR to conference room 412, the man was surprised by a rousing round of applause and congratulations from his new on-purpose pals. After brief individual greetings with each, the Professor called them all to order. Everyone took chairs around a conference table.

"Welcome," said the Professor, greeting the group. Turning to the man he said, "This is your first *Gathering*."

"What a pleasant surprise!" the man exclaimed. "I have everyone in this room to thank for helping me become an On-Purpose Person."

The Professor began, "Gatherings are regular meetings to review each others' respective progress, to encourage and support one another, and to have mutual accountability. A Gathering can be two or more On-Purpose Persons, called Gathering Partners. We combined small groups for your commencement.

"Here's a copy of the *Gathering Agenda*, a simple format used to review our weekly progress.[1]

"The Gathering Agenda is in sections—On-Purpose Statements, Giving, and Transformation. It can be a quick check-in needing only about fifteen minutes. Some Gatherings elect to meet longer."

The high school student said, "Each Gathering begins by reading aloud Ecclesiastes 3:1–2. This helps us view the bigger perspective of what season we're in today."

The homemaker added, "We review our On-Purpose Plans—core wants, purpose, vision, and mission statements—and our giving to focus us on what we've said is truly important."

Betty Rose spoke: "Next, we answer the questions provided as springboards for discussions of current matters. It isn't necessary to answer each question. They're aids to jog our thoughts."

John, the pastor, interjected, "The next item is giving. We make sure we haven't fallen victim to being too self-centered. By the way, confidentiality is a must for the group to be a safe place to share concerns and joys, and to review and discuss our on-purpose successes and failures."

Bob Scott said, "It's also a time to seek and give feedback, accountability, and encouragement. We openly share our lives and plans for the coming week."

"Relationships are built in your Gathering partnerships," Perry added. "The power of peers is highly beneficial because the collective experience, perspective, energy, resources, and support sharpen our thinking. No longer are we alone with our thoughts. The Gathering provides a regular source for innovation, development, and growth. By tapping into your partners' wisdom and encouragement, your batting average is sure to rise."

"Sharing," said the Professor, "strengthens us. Open the door to others to become an On-Purpose Person. Who do you know who's ready to benefit from being on-purpose? Sometimes the best

---

1 See Appendix for the complete Gathering Agenda.

we can do is plant the seed of the approach. Some time ago an On-Purpose Person gave you my name. When the time was right, you remembered, and you sought me out. There's what we call the On-Purpose Person's paradox—the more you serve others, the more refined becomes your understanding of yourself and purpose. Helping others truly helps you."

The man smiled. "It amazes me. I start by writing down all that I want, and I end up making a difference for others from my strengths. It is a paradox."

The Professor said, "When sharing the On-Purpose Approach, give it freely. Your purpose, if hoarded, will wither. Instead, go deep with your purpose so it can thrive, grow, and transform you. From this strength, you can give to others. That is the essence of the next stage—becoming an On-Purpose Leader.

"At this point, continue solidifying your purpose, vision, missions, and values. You can't share what you don't have. Invest the time, effort, and energy to be on-purpose. Giving will naturally flow from the abundance found in being on-purpose. In this manner, giving is deeply authentic."

The man understood. "Thank you for your wise counsel. Allowing my purpose to take root in my life is my focus for now. I'm still so new at this."

As a novice at being on-purpose, he anticipated it would take time to turn on the light switch in every life account. The progressive integration of his purpose into his everyday life was a commencement exercise—the beginning of becoming an on-purpose person.

Before the close of the Gathering, the Professor made a point of taking aside Perry, the business consultant and executive coach, for a brief discussion. Perry then approached the man and said, "The Professor and I agree that it makes sense for you to join my Gathering. Interested?"

"Yes! I would like that," the man immediately agreed.

They had an in-depth discussion of respective expectations and commitments. Gathering partnerships, Perry explained, are not one-way arrangements. He would introduce the man to the two other men in the Gathering. The man would have Gathering Partners.

THE REWARD

We never know how high we are
Till we are called to rise
And then, if we are true to plan,
Our statures touch the skies.

—Emily Dickinson (1830–1886)

CHAPTER 19

True Success

We are here to be excited
from youth to old age,
to have an insatiable curiosity
about the world . . .
We are also here to help others
by practicing a friendly attitude.
And every person
is born for a purpose.
Everyone has a God-given
potential, in essence,
built into them.
And if we are to live life
to its fullest,
we must realize that potential.

—Norman Vincent Peale (1898–1993)
Pastor and author, The Power of Positive Thinking

YEARS HAD PASSED since the man's first Gathering in that college conference room. Now he was known throughout his community as a man of extraordinary contribution, faith, and character.

Being on-purpose was integrated into every aspect of his life. He applied the principles and process with increasing skill and results. Decisions were consistent with his purpose. Every year since that first year, he annually set aside time to create an On-Purpose Plan. His purpose was the cornerstone of his life and work.

He was in Perry's Gathering for a few years. Eventually, circumstances changed so that they no longer met regularly, but they remained in contact. The man shared the On-Purpose Approach with his best friend and they became Gathering Partners. In time, they shared the Approach with others and mentored them. As a result of the man's original Gathering partnership with Perry branching out, and then those groups branching out again and again, literally hundreds of people were On-Purpose Persons in creation. Gatherings were taking place at schools, churches, businesses, and homes. Thousands of lives were being touched and transformed as individuals were discovering their purpose and living on-purpose. As a community they encouraged and cared for one another.

The man's wife witnessed the transformation in his life and in their marriage. He shared the On-Purpose Approach with her. She invited a friend to be her Gathering Partner. This Gathering grew to include more women. It, too, branched out, giving birth to Gatherings for women.

Life was still not fair. The "river current" still provided rapids and whirlpools that surprised him, but they didn't shake him. These trials became times of transition, strengthening, and growth—an essential aspect of life. He navigated through them with his purpose and Gathering Partners as compass and crew, respectively.

The man's self-worth had grown—and so had his financial net worth. Relationships with family, friends, business associates, and neighbors were positive, productive, and fulfilling.

He prospered materially, eventually becoming the president of the company, but money and status no longer drove his life. When he stopped chasing worldly success and reordered his life to be on-purpose, his wants were plentifully met. A point came when he realized he had enough. From this overflow, he became a generous giver—giving away much more than the basic 10 percent.

Periodically, he would open and review his notes from his first year of being on-purpose. It amazed him how many of his wants were realized. Even more amazing was how his present wants were so much deeper and fuller than he could even have imagined back then. He was humbled and thankful to see the significance of his life as it was being used in the creation.

He truly was a man who, with the help of others, was creating a meaningful life integrated by his purpose and living into his unique design and understanding of true success. He was finishing strong. The On-Purpose Person Program worked!

• • •

One afternoon, as he prepared to leave the office for home, his cell phone rang. Answering it, he was greeted by a young man's voice: "Sir, I'm not quite sure why I'm calling you. A former professor of mine from college said you are known as an On-Purpose Person. He gave me your cell phone number and recommended I call you. I'm trying to figure out what I should do with my life. I'm torn in so many directions and overwhelmed. I need direction in my life. My professor said you might be willing to share with me what it means to be an On-Purpose Person. Can you help me make my life make sense?"

A smile stretched across the man's face. "Yes, let's meet at my office tomorrow! The Professor told me to expect a call from a fine young man who is his former student. I know your situation more than you know." His pulse quickened with excitement—an opportunity to help another person discover his purpose and to be an On-Purpose Person!

This is what it means to be on-purpose. The man had truly become an On-Purpose Person.

Appendix

THE ON-PURPOSE PERSON WEEKLY GATHERING AGENDA

Begin by reading the following passage aloud together:

To everything there is a season,
A time for every purpose under heaven:
A time to be born,
    And a time to die;
A time to plant,
    And a time to pluck up what is planted.
(Ecclesiastes 3:1-2)

From Ecclesiastes, I identify the current "season" of my life as being a time to . . . Why?

I do/don't see a change in season . . .

ON-PURPOSE STATEMENTS

Open your On-Purpose Folder, review, and read your On-Purpose Statements.

Next, within the Gathering, openly respond to the appropriate questions.

I have most recently achieved these items on my want list . . .

If I feel off-purpose, I need to make these changes to be on-purpose . . .

The recent day that was closest to an Ideal On-Purpose Day was . . . Why?

The recent day that was most off-purpose was . . . Why?

I made an intentional choice that moved me from off-purpose to on-purpose. It was . . .

These impediments are preventing me from being on-purpose . . .

I am doing this to remove them . . .

My on-purpose batting average did/didn't improve . . .

To prepare and equip myself for being on-purpose I have undertaken the following actions . . .

I had . . . (state number) opportunities to review my On-Purpose Folder during the past week.

My most on-purpose moment was . . . Why?

My most off-purpose moment was . . . Why?

The following recent experiences tested the passion of my purpose . . .

In the coming days I face the following challenges and opportunities to my being an On-Purpose Person . . .

GIVING

I have/haven't given joyfully, intentionally, and proportionately according to my means . . .

I have/haven't given from all three areas: time, talent, and resources . . .

My giving has/hasn't been consistent with my give list . . .

TRANSFORMATION

I believe the following person would benefit from knowing about the On-Purpose Person Program . . .

I shared or introduced the concepts of the On-Purpose Person with this person . . .

This will be my follow-up action . . .

CONCLUSION

Each week read one quote from the beginning of a chapter in *The On-Purpose Person*. Discuss it.

Acknowledgments

Writing a book is a monumental challenge. Although the author is on center stage, many people behind the scenes contribute in their own personal, special manner. In a sense, it becomes a group effort. I'd like to thank my cast and crew:

Special thanks are given to the Rev. Paul Crowell for wielding his red pen on early drafts of the original book that resulted in greater clarity of thought and ease of reading. In this updated version, my business partner, Mary Tomlinson, similarly offered detailed insights and suggestions based on her extensive use of the book with coaching clients.

A special tribute goes to Betty Pratt, Jay "Dr. J" Brophy, Perry Nies, and H. David Wilson. These on-purpose persons provided measures of inspiration for characters in the book.

For the reading of early drafts and encouragement along the way, many thanks to Steve Levée, Jane and Perry Nies, Shirley Pipkin, John Budlong, George Romot, Harry Griffith, Alan Welsh, Denny Johnson, Frank Attwood, Dr. Ron Behner, John Smith, Rev. Peter Moore, Roger Stitt, my CEO group, Vicky McVay, Murray Fisher, Tom Downs, Walter Walker, and Thayer Bigelow.

This latest version of the book benefited from reading by Kirk Squires, Janet Cronstedt, Jim Esch, and Tony Clark.

Thank you to Bob Smith of American Reprographics in Winter Park, Florida, for your guidance, printing, and binding of my original self-published books. Truly, your service is legendary! Your children continue your indelible legacy.

Becky Kaiser provided editing and typing for much of the original manuscript. Julie Holzmann helped with proofing and cleanups of this updated book. Her patient reading and rereading has polished the text and pushed me to be a better writer.

Piñon Press was a tremendous partner as the publisher of the early editions. A nicer, more professional, and competent team could not have been handpicked. Nancy Burke was consistently a joyful and ready helper. Bruce Nygren shared the vision and possibilities immediately. He was the editorial director, project leader, guide, and friend. His willingness to listen, patience, and sound suggestions led to key improvements in the manuscript. Dean Galiano, the special markets manager at Navpress in the 1990s, continues to be a friend and has single-handedly sold more books than anyone. John Eames, Mark Kuyper, Kent Wilson, and Paul Santhouse, all members of the original Navpress team, remain friends through the years. Reflecting upon their respective careers today, I count my blessings for such a remarkably talented team surrounding a novice author many years ago.

Greenleaf Book Group has taken the 2009 book to a more contemporary feel and look. Clint Greenleaf and Meg La Borde have assembled a talented team that includes Justin Branch, Alan Grimes, Lisa Woods, and Matthew Donnelley.

Creative kudos go to Barbara Georgoudiou who designed our new On-Purpose® logo and graphics package that has heavily influenced the new book packaging, fonts, and interior layouts. Her art director ability offers both artistic input and comfort for a guy like me whose eye for design is admittedly suspect.

My parents and brother, Bob, were there for me in the formative years of my life. They encouraged me and allowed me to learn life's lessons. I've never felt more appreciation and love than I do today for the blessings they are in my life.

Having over 200,000 copies of the original book in worldwide circulation translates into too many readers to cite who have commented and shared insights that have informed and inspired me. Of special note are David Zerfoss, Gordie Allen, Bill Stewart, John White, Roey Diefendorf, Regi Campbell, Tom Haynes and Brenda Standlee. I'm learning from them constantly, so "Thank you."

I want to thank my wife, Judith, from whom I never heard a discouraging word during the term of this writing project. She is my best friend and my love.

Foremost, I want to thank God for the life experiences, giftedness, and inspiration that led to and enabled the co-creation of this book—his handiwork through me has blessed me richly.

—Kevin W. McCarthy

On-Purpose® Resources
The difference in people who make a difference!™

Are you ready to be yourself, to prosper, and to make a difference? Your best first step is to sign-up for a free subscription to The On-Purpose® Minutes: twice a week short videos by Kevin McCarthy that will help you to become an on-purpose person at home and at work.

Explore the possibilities of being on-purpose through a variety of learning experiences, products, and services. Visit the On-Purpose family of web sites to learn more:

Subscribe here: www.kevinwmccarthy.com
Explore here: www.on-purpose.com
Meet here: www.onpurposeplanet.com
Work here: www.onpurposeatwork.com

Please write or call us at:
On-Purpose Partners, LLC
PO Box 1568
Winter Park, FL 32790-1568
Phone: 407.657.6000
Email: info@on-purpose.com

SPECIAL OFFER: Forms for the Want List and Tournament method presented in Chapters 4–6 are available as a free e-book download. Go to www.discoveryguide.net to get it.

About the Author

Kevin is the first to tell you he's an unlikely author. In the late 1980s, this businessman, now business advisor, observed unproductive patterns of thinking and behaviors in clients' lives, work, and businesses that disadvantaged them strategically and competitively. At the core was the absence of a strong sense of self and identity. Kevin set out to help his clients and himself think more clearly and make better decisions. His focus rested on the concept of knowing one's purpose and the alignment of one's life with it. The roots of The On-Purpose® Approach were born.

This lifetime entrepreneur is classically trained in business. The typical track for best-selling authors rarely involves a business career, yet Kevin holds his Bachelor of Science degree in Business and Economics from Lehigh University and his Masters of Business Administration (MBA) from The Darden School at the University of Virginia. He grew up in Pittsburgh, PA and attended Shady Side Academy where he was the perennial class president.

In business, Kevin fully expected to be the business manager of a talented inventor, artist, or personality. He didn't anticipate himself becoming the face and voice of a greater message. For decades, this pioneer of the On-Purpose® message and methods has written, spoken, and advised clients in strategy for life and business.

The story in *The On-Purpose Person* is fictional, yet every author reveals a bit of himself in every book. Kevin regularly reminds us that authors write most about their struggles and that he is not the on-purpose person. He's simply the author of a book with the same title and he's a man working through the trials and joys of life more strategically thanks to the On-Purpose® perspective.

Kevin and Judith, his bride since 1984, live in Winter Park, Florida, USA along with their two children, Charles and Anne.